# PRESCHOOL CHILDREN WITH WORKING PARENTS

## An Analysis of Attachment Relationships

## Nancy Boyd Webb

UNIVERSITY
PRESS OF
AMERICA

LANHAM • NEW YORK • LONDON

Copyright © 1984 by

University Press of America,™ Inc.

4720 Boston Way
Lanham. MD 20706

3 Henrietta Street
London WC2E 8LU England

Library of Congress Cataloging in Publication Data

Webb, Nancy Boyd, 1932-
  Preschool children with working parents.

  Bibliography: p.
  Includes index.
  1. Children of working parents—United States.
2. Parent and child—United States. 3. Attachment behav-
ior. 4. Child rearing—United States. 5. Child care
workers—United States. 6. Day care centers—United
States. I. Title.
HQ777.6.W42   1984      649'.123      84-13042
ISBN 0-8191-4169-0 (alk. paper)
ISBN 0-8191-4170-4 (pbk. : alk. paper)


All University Press of America books are produced on acid-free
paper which exceeds the minimum standards set by the National
Historical Publications and Records Commission.

# TABLE OF CONTENTS

# LIST OF TABLES

I    PRESCHOOLERS

THEIR WORKING PARENTS

AND VARIOUS CARETAKERS

Chapter One

# THE YOUNG CHILD COPES WITH THE WORK-A-DAY WORLD

The life of a preschool child in the 1980's differs drastically from the childhood of his parents and grandparents. Older generations recall nostalgic memories of carefree play around their neighborhoods, while Mother baked cookies in the kitchen and was ready to bandage a skinned knee and wipe away the accompanying tears. These warm associations of yesteryear will not be shared by most youngsters raised in the 1970's and 1980's. The world of <u>Where Did You Go? Out. What Did You Do? Nothing.</u>[1] assumed a pattern of family life which permitted the child to roam within the neighborhood and return to home base at will, since somebody (usually Mother) was home waiting for the child's eventual return.

With increasing numbers of working mothers, and diverse provisions for child care out of the home, many preschoolers themselves spend relatively little time at home any more. Their routine often includes a daily commute to day care or nursery school, and additional hours spent with relatives, neighbors, and other sitters who fill in for the parents before and after day care hours. The child learns at an early age that there are <u>many</u> caretakers, besides Mother, who can put on Band-Aids and wipe away tears.

The following story has numerous versions. Its theme is played with different variations in the homes of more than six million preschoolers in the United States who have working mothers. This fictitious family is a composite of many families, but the details of their life are familiar to many whose daily experiences are similar.

## The Daily Grind: One Child's Day

Once upon a time there was a quiet suburban community located about twenty-five miles from a major metropolitan area in Northeastern United States. Let's call the town  Edenwood and the family heroes of our story, the Armstrongs. The Armstrongs are what used to be called a typical "average American family," consisting of a mother, a father, and two children: a boy, Adam, age four; and a girl, Eve, age six.

It is a January morning. The alarm goes off at
5:30 a.m. Mrs. Armstrong gets up quietly, dresses in
the dark, re-sets the alarm for 6:30 and goes downstairs. There she makes coffee, sets the table for
four and then sits down and eats breakfast alone. She
leaves the house by 6:15 to get to the hospital by 6:45
where she works as a nurse on the 7-to-3 shift.

At 6:30 the alarm goes off again and Mr. Armstrong
gets up, wakes Adam and Eve, and begins getting dressed.
Adam brushes his teeth and watches his father shave,
while Eve tries to get her father's attention by asking
him which of two new toys she received for her birthday
she should take to school for Show and Tell. Mr. Armstrong suggests she take one today and one tomorrow,
and then he tells both children to hurry and finish
dressing. He follows Eve into her room where he
brushes her hair and lets her choose which color barrette she wants to wear.

After cereal and milk the family leaves the house
together around 7:30. Eve kisses her father goodbye
and walks alone two houses down the street where she
goes in the back door and waits with her friend, Rachel,
until 8:15 when it is time for them to leave for school
together. Eve will return to Rachel's house after
school and remain there until her mother picks her up
sometime between 3:45 and 4:30 (depending on how many
errands Mrs. Armstrong has to do after work).

Meanwhile, Mr. Armstrong and Adam drive to the day
care center where Mr. Armstrong parks the car and accompanies his son into the building. After helping
Adam off with his jacket, Mr. Armstrong begins his
daily forty-five minute commute to his job in the city.
It is 8:00 a.m. and the road is crowded as usual with
other commuters.

Adam spends eight hours per day, five days per
week at the day care center, where approximately half
of the fourteen children in his "group" have been his
classmates for over one year. Adam's forty-hour week
at day care equals the time his parents spend at their
jobs. On Saturdays Adam goes with his sister to his
maternal grandparents for the day, while his mother
attends Saturday college, and his father works on a
second job in his father-in-law's business. Mrs.
Armstrong is studying for an additional nursing degree.

The parents want to buy their own home and are trying to save for the down payment.

The children's time with their parents is limited to an hour alone with their father in the morning five days a week; approximately three hours per day alone with their mother (in the late afternoon from 4 to 7); and one-and-a-half to two hours per day with both parents together before bedtime. On Saturday Adam and Eve enjoy playing together and with their cousins at their grandparents' house. They see no more of their parents on Saturdays than on regular weekdays, but on Sunday the family spends most of the day together, occupied with never-ending routine household chores interspersed with deliberate attempts on both parents' parts to spend some time individually with each child.

## Demographic Facts of Life: Present Reality and Future Trends

Preschoolers growing up in the 1980's are experiencing a completely new and different world from the one in which most of their parents were raised. Whereas care of preschool children in the United States traditionally was a home-based, maternal function, in recent years child caring has changed drastically from the exclusive one-to-one relationship of mother and child. Numerous caretakers, both within the home and in institutions such as preschool programs and day care centers, now share the child caring role with the parents and other relatives.

Working Mothers. Employment of women, including mothers of school-age children, has risen steadily and sharply since the end of World War II. This trend is especially dramatic among mothers of preschool children, and within this group the fastest growing segment is mothers with children under age two.[2] Between 1950 and 1976 the employment rate among mothers of preschool children nearly tripled, climbing from eleven to thirty-seven percent.[3] It is now estimated to be about fifty percent. Projections for 1990 envision a seventy percent labor force participation among women aged twenty-five to fifty-four,[4] millions of whom inevitably will be mothers of children under age six.

Although preschool children have always received some care from relatives and other caretakers in addition to their mothers, the need for such arrangements

on a regular basis is critical when both parents, or
the custodial parent in a divorced or separated family,
works. The tremendous increase in one-parent families
has contributed significantly to the rise in female out-
of-home employment, with custodial mothers and fathers
of young children relying strongly on alternative child
care to supplement their work-related absences from
their children. While only about half of the children
in two-parent families need supplemental care (beyond
that provided by the parents), two-thirds of those in
single parent families require such care.[5] Growing up
with working parents means for most children in the
1980's growing up with multiple caretakers.

Child Care Arrangements. Working parents of preschool
children have many options in selecting care for their
children. The choices include care in their own home
or in a sitter's home, care provided by a relative or
non-relative, and enrolling the child in some form of
preschool program such as nursery school or day care.
Economic and value considerations inevitably enter into
the type of care selected, as does the age of the child
and the availability and quality of specific programs
and caretakers within any one family's social and community network.

Demographers and social historians have a difficult
and frustrating task as they try to obtain and interpret
statistics about the care parents actually select for
their preschool children. Jessie Bernard (1974) maintains that "adequate state and local data on child care
arrangements are almost totally nonexistent"[6] and Sheila
Kamerman (1980) laments that "data are not collected
systematically and in one place" nor are data "disag-
gregated for working mothers."[7]

Because of these limitations, analyses of child
care arrangements based primarily on census data probably do not reflect an accurate picture. For example,
a 1974 and 1975 census bureau report indicated that even
parents of preschoolers whose mothers work full-time
consider themselves the primary caretakers of their
children.[8] In view of the fact that only one-fifth
to one-third of working parents arrange their work
hours so that one or the other is available to provide
child care,[9] it is not clear how the remaining four-
fifths to two-thirds could manage without using supple-
mentary caretakers, in addition to a preschool program.

Parents obviously want to stress the importance of their role, and they conceivably may minimize the involvement of other caretakers, especially in reporting to the census.

Several recent in-depth studies of working families portray diverse caretaking patterns for preschool children.[10] Kamerman's study of over two hundred families with working mothers found that more than half of the sample of preschool children experienced two or more types of care each week (one of which often was a preschool program), while the other half received three or four types of routine care on a weekly basis. Kamerman comments that

> child care, for working parents, means packaging a variety of care modes. The packages often include both in-home and out-of-home care and may even include multiple arrangements, with two types of out-of-home care (group and family day care), as well as two or more arrangements at home, used to care for one child in the course of a week. The amount and extent of parental ingenuity and creativeness are extraordinary, with parents sometimes selecting complicated work schedules in order to provide a significant portion of child care themselves.[11]

There are probably few, if any, preschool children in the United States today who have been raised exclusively by one caretaker. It is hard to imagine a totally exclusive child-rearing situation. Multiple caretaking, thus, is a matter of degree, ranging from the single-parent mother supported on welfare—who only occasionally utilizes a baby-sitter or neighbor for back-up child care, to the intact family with both parents working whose child is in full-time day care and involved with a variety of caretakers in addition to the parents.

A trend toward utilizing some form of preschool program for children aged three to five, whether their mothers work or not, has been increasing steadily in recent years. (The term "preschool program" refers to half-day nursery school and other short-term institutional programs which the child attends for part of the

7

day, several days per week.)  Parents enroll their
children in these programs because they anticipate edu-
cational and socialization benefits for the child, and/
or because they want or need some free time for themselves.

In 1967 only six percent of three-year-olds were
enrolled in preschool programs, but by 1976 this percentage had risen to twenty percent.  The enrollment
for four-year-olds doubled (from twenty-one to forty-one
percent) during the same period, and the percentage for
five-year-olds climbed from sixty-five to eighty-one
percent.[12]  Enrollment of all age groups undoubtedly
has increased substantially since 1976, particularly
among the younger children.  Kamerman's analysis of the
best available national statistics as of 1980 suggests
that about sixty-four percent of children aged three to
five are in some form of school or out-of-home care program, whether their mothers work or not.[13]

Until recently, entry into preschool programs such
as nursery school was not common before the child's
third birthday, when toilet training usually is established and many parents and child care specialists
believe that the child tolerates separation more easily.
In response to the increased needs of working parents,
it is now possible in most communities to obtain a
range of child care options, including the following:

- Infant day care (care of babies in a
  group setting),
- Family day care (care of babies and
  children in the home of a non-
  relative),
- "Regular" day care (day-long group
  care with meals and naps on a five-
  day-per-week basis),
- Individual arrangements (care by a
  relative or non-related sitter in
  the child's or caretaker's home).

A study of actual usage of various methods of care
in 1976 (the Unco Survey)[14] revealed that in families
with working mothers with children under the age of six
about forty percent arrange for child care in the home
of a relative or non-relative, while about twenty-nine
percent have the caretaker come to their own home.  Care
by relatives and by non-relatives occurs with similar

frequency (thirty-one percent - relatives and thirty-eight percent - non-relatives). Approximately eighteen percent of families utilized nursery schools and day care centers, and the remaining parents indicated that they, themselves, serve as their children's prime source of care.

Participation of fathers in routine child care has made a tremendous difference in the ability and willingness of many mothers to leave home and join the labor force. This will be discussed more fully in Part II as one of five distinct caretaking patterns among working parents. Involvement of relatives, especially grandparents, has also facilitated maternal labor force participation. Relatives, who sometimes refuse to accept payment for their services, therefore make the mother's working more lucrative for the family.

Comparative costs of different child care alternatives often weigh significantly in the kind of care selected by families. A 1982 analysis of child care trends[15] indicated that among the half of working families which pay for child care arrangements, care in the parents' home by a relative amounts to about $1,000 yearly as compared to about $2,000 for care in a center. Purchase of out-of-home care by a non-relative is the costliest alternative, with center care next, and in-home care by a non-relative third. These costs vary greatly depending on the child's age, and on various geographic locations around the country.

While both families and schools (including pre-school programs) continue to play a major role as caretakers of American children, "the overwhelming majority of families supplement parental and school care with at least one, and usually more than one, regular non-parental care arrangement."[16] This was the conclusion of a report by Mary Jo Bane in 1979 summarizing four national surveys on care of children under the age of fourteen. This statistic applies both to families in which mothers work outside the home and where they stay home. Obviously the need for non-parental caretakers is more acute in families of working parents.

Whether care is given at home, or in a group setting, and whether by relatives or by unrelated caretakers, the sheer fact of increased numbers of working mothers means that more and more children are receiving

9

care from non-maternal caretakers. We need to know more about the quality of the relationships the child forms with these "substitute mothers." Indeed, we need to know if the child forms attachment bonds to them and what effect, if any, these other relationships have on the child's relationship with the parents. Exploration of this important issue was a primary goal motivating the research on which this book is based.

## Implications of Daily Separations and Multiple Caretakers on Attachment Formation

Far from being eternal verities, attitudes about motherhood and about childrearing change with time and reflect the prevailing social mores of different eras. For example, an 1898 publication titled Ideal Motherhood warns mothers as follows about relinquishing the care of their children to "hirelings":

> The children's nurses in stately
> homes are sometimes more truly the
> mothers of the little ones they watch
> and tend than the women who love them.
> The woman who delegates the entire
> care of her children to hirelings, no
> matter how wisely chosen, misses the
> best that can be given to her, and
> sells her divine birthright of mother-
> hood for empty glitter and excitement. [17]

By 1970 views about childrearing had changed so completely that social historian Philip Slater felt compelled to expose what he termed "the magnification of motherhood"[18] among post World War II middle-class American housewives. According to Slater, Benjamin Spock contributed to the inflation of the importance of motherhood by implying (in his 1968 edition) that only a full-time mother could avoid bringing up a child who would become a social problem.[19]

In the seventy years between Ideal Motherhood and Philip Slater a virtual deluge of research and publications by psychologists, psychiatrists and child development specialists emphasized and re-emphasized the persisting and critical effects of early experience and the mother-child interaction, in particular, on subsequent development. Sigmund Freud,[20] Leon Yarrow,[21] and

10

Selma Fraiberg,[22] among many others, singled out the mother-child relationship as the unique prototype of all later love relationships, and hence fueled fires of smoldering worry among mothers who thenceforth felt a tremendous burden of psychological responsibility connected to the task of bringing up their babies.

John Bowlby's writings about attachment in 1958 and 1969[23] added yet more scientific fuel to the public's growing conviction that the mother's role was crucially significant for the healthy development of the young child. Although Bowlby's theory of attachment was based on the belief that the child's tendency to attach was instinctive and served the purpose of survival, whereas the psychoanalytic and social learning view was that the child becomes attached to the ministering person because of need satisfaction and the reinforcement of pleasure, the end result of both positions was the same: establishment of the exquisite, and near-exclusive importance of the mother-child relationship on human development as a tenet, the breaching of which threatens terrible risks.

Beatrice Whiting, the Harvard anthropologist who edited the book, Six Cultures—Studies of Child Rearing,[24] points out that American culture ranks far above other societies in the value we place on the mother's presence at home with the children all or most of the time. What happens when economic necessity forces the mother to take a job which prevents her from seeing her child except for a few hours a day? Selma Fraiberg in Every Child's Birthright[25] warned that the children of working mothers cared for by numerous caretakers might fail to form the attachment bonds necessary for healthy emotional and cognitive development. The question explored and discussed in the research study reported here is whether the attachment to the mother will become "diluted," compromised, or changed because of competing, and possibly numerous, attachments to other caretakers.

By "attachment" we mean "an affectional bond, enduring in nature, and specific in its focus."[26] Since we cannot see these bonds, we infer their existence by observing certain behaviors which have come to be considered "hallmarks of attachment."[27] These are:

1. proximity-seeking and proximity-maintaining behaviors, and
2. responses of protest upon separation.

11

Examples of attachment behavior are the close following of the mother by the toddling child and the despairing cries of anger and outrage when the mother goes away and the child is prevented from accompanying her. Prior to toddler-hood, the baby, who cannot as yet physically follow the mother, nonetheless manages to bring her to his side via cries and vocalizations. The baby, thus, enhances the mutual bonding process by smiling and by clinging to this person who embodies for him the essence of protection, security, and survival.

Bowlby believes that "attachment behavior becomes directed primarily towards one person and (that) the child becomes strongly possessive of that person."[28] Readiness to form attachments is especially strong during the fourth, fifth, and sixth months of life, and by six months of age most children show signs of attachment,[29] as evidenced in attempts to maintain proximity with the loved person, and by protesting (usually by crying) when separated from that person.

Bowlby states that "almost from the first, many children have more than one figure towards whom they direct attachment behavior; (however) these figures are not treated alike...by twelve months a plurality of attachment figures is probably the rule, (but) these figures are not treated as the equivalents of one another."[30] The primary caretaker is considered by Bowlby to hold a very special place in the child's affections, distinct from his attachments to others. Michael Rutter, another British psychiatrist, believes that up to four or five substitute caretaking figures can be tolerated in early childhood "if the mothering is of high quality and is provided by figures who remain the same during the child's early life."[31]

Working parents usually cannot guarantee this continuity of "high quality" caretaking by a few stable individuals. Even if they could do so, anthropologists suggest that it may not be advisable. Margaret Mead stated in 1954 that "cross-cultural studies suggest that adjustment is most facilitated if the child is cared for by many warm friendly people"[32] (emphasis mine). In 1962 Mead argued that children with multiple caretakers may actually be better off than the child involved in a mother-child pair relationship which, because of its exclusivity, predisposes the child to trauma if this key relationship is disturbed by separation.[33]

Daily separations are an inevitable occurrence when the mother of a young child goes to work. We need to know if and how these separations affect the "key" mother-child relationship. Similarly, substitute caretakers inevitably must fill in for the mother while she is away, and we need to know about the nature of the child's ensuing relationships with these various substitute caretakers, and about how these relationships compare to the bond between the child and the mother.

## Focus and Main Themes of Book

This book analyzes the daily lives of a group of preschool children of working parents. It focuses on the children's relationships with their parents and their other regular caretakers, and highlights advantages for the children resulting from their multiple caretaking experiences.

Contrary to Fraiberg's warning, the group of children on which this book is based attached firmly to their parents, despite extensive multiple caretaking and the minimal involvement of their parents in their day-to-day care. The book analyzes the <u>unique characteristics of the parent-child interaction</u> which enable it to withstand the rigors of repeated, protracted daily separations, and which serve to perpetuate attachment bonds. The book also highlights the <u>advantages</u> to the child of <u>early socialization</u> experiences resulting from group care beyond the nuclear family. These are evident in peer bonds, early group experience and extra-familial adult-child relationships.

NOTES

1. Smith, Robert P., <u>Where Did You Go? Out. What Did You Do? Nothing.</u> (New York: Norton) 1968 ed. reproduction of 1958.

2. Zigler, Edward F. and Gordon, Edmund W., eds. <u>Day Care</u> (Boston: Auburn House Publishing Company) 1982, p.v.

3. U.S. Bureau of the Census, <u>Statistical Abstract of the United States: 1977</u> (98th edition) p. 392.

4. Kamerman, Sheila B., <u>Parenting in an Unresponsive Society</u> (New York: The Free Press), 1980, p. 9; and Rowe, Mary, "Choosing Child Care: Many Options" in <u>Working Couples</u> (eds.) Robert and Rhona Rapaport (New York: Harper Colophon Books) 1978, p. 89.

5. Winget, W. Gary, "The Dilemma of Affordable Child Care" in Zigler and Gordon, op. cit., p. 353.

6. Bernard, Jessie, <u>The Future of Motherhood</u> (New York: Penguin Books) 1974, p. 399.

7. Kamerman, p. 33.

8. Bane, Mary Jo et.al., "Child-care arrangements of working parents," <u>Monthly Labor Review</u>, October 1979, p. 51.

9. Ibid., and Rowe, p. 92.

10. See, especially, Kamerman, <u>op. cit.</u> and "The Working Family Project" in <u>Working Couples</u> (eds.) Robert and Rhona Rapaport (New York: Harper Colophon) 1978, pp. 74-87, and Webb, Nancy B., "Attachment Relationships of Preschoolers to Parents and Other Familiar Caretakers: Implications for Day Care and Working Mothers," unpublished D.S.W. dissertation, Columbia University, 1979, pp. 145-154.

11. Kamerman, p. 36.

12. Bane, p. 52. The large number of five-year-olds enrolled in preschool programs reflects increasing kindergarten registration.

13. Kamerman, p. 33.

14. Unco, Inc., <u>National Child Consumer Study</u>: 1975,
    Vol. 2 Washington, D.C.: U.S. Department of Health,
    Education and Welfare, Office of Child Development,
    prepared under contract #105-74-1107, 1976.

15. Winget, <u>op. cit.</u>, pp. 354-355.

16. Bane, p. 52.

17. Davis, Minnie, <u>Ideal Motherhood</u> (Boston: Crowell)
    1898, p. 29.

18. Slater, Philip, <u>The Pursuit of Loneliness</u> (Boston:
    Beacon Press), 1970.

19. Ibid., p. 64.

20. Freud, Sigmund, <u>An Outline of Psychoanalysis</u>
    (London: Hogarth) 1938, p. 188.

21. Yarrow, Leon, "The Development of Focused Rela-
    tionships During Infancy," in <u>Exceptional Infant</u> I,
    (1967) p. 429.

22. Fraiberg, Selma, "The Origin of Human Bonds,"
    <u>Commentary</u>, December, 1969, pp. 45-57.

23. Bowlby, John, "The Nature of the Child's Tie to His
    Mother," <u>International Journal of Psycho-Analysis</u>,
    39 (1958): 350-373 and Attachment and Loss, Vol. 1:
    <u>Attachment</u>, (New York: Pelican) 1969.

24. Whiting, Beatrice, ed. <u>Six Cultures--Studies of
    Child Rearing</u> (New York: John Wiley and Sons) 1963.
    Whiting's views about the role of the American
    mother were given in a paper, "The American Family:
    A Cross Cultural Perspective," presented at the
    Harvard Alumni College, Cambridge, Mass., 11 July
    1978.

25. Fraiberg, Selma, <u>Every Child's Birthright: In
    Defense of Mothering</u> (New York: Basic Books) 1977.

26. Lamb, Michael, "A Defense of the Concept of Attach-
    ment," <u>Human Development</u>, 17 (1974) p. 376.

27. Ibid., and
Ainsworth, Mary, "Attachment and Dependency: A
Comparison," in <u>Attachment and Dependency</u>, ed.
J. Gerwirtz (Washington, D.C.: Winston, 1972) p. 102.

28. Bowlby, J., <u>Attachment</u>, p. 368.

29. Ibid., p. 383. The issue of a "critical period"
for attachment formation is complex and still under
study and debate.

30. Ibid., pp. 362-363.

31. Rutter, Michael, <u>Maternal Deprivation Reassessed</u>
(Baltimore: Penguin Books) 1972, p. 25.

32. Mead Margaret, "Some Theoretical Considerations on
the Problem of Mother-Child Separation," <u>American
Journal of Orthopsychiatry</u> 24 (1954): 477.

33. Mead, Margaret, "A Cultural Anthropologist's
Approach to Maternal Deprivation," <u>Deprivation of
Maternal Care</u>, ed. Mary Ainsworth (Geneva, WHO,
1962) p. 56.

## Chapter Two

## PRESCHOOLERS AND THEIR CARETAKERS

How does one study the relationships of children with their various caretakers? Will a child who spends eight hours a day with a baby-sitter feel closer bonds of affection toward the sitter than to his mother whom he sees for only half that time? What about the child's relationship with his grandparents, with whom he spends every Saturday, and talks on the phone several times a week? How do these interactions compare with the child's relationship with the day care teacher with whom the child has spent forty hours per week over the past two years? How do all these relationships with multiple caretakers affect the basic parent-child at-tachment relationship?

The research upon which this book is based em-ployed three different research methods to explore these questions:

- Projective Doll Play Interviews
- Caretaker Questionnaires
- Participant Observations

After outlining how the research was done (The Study Design), this chapter will describe the families which participated in the project (The Study Sample).

### The Study Design

Analyzing the nature and quality of a child's attachment relationships is a complex process, requir-ing a multi-faceted approach. The most direct method would be to ask the caretakers and the children how they get along and how they feel about each other. This ap-proach is deceptively simple, however, since people often have difficulty expressing their feelings, and asking a young child to choose preferred caretakers is probably beyond his ability and, even if possible, would risk the resentment of the adults involved with the child.

A Projective Doll Play Interview avoided this con-flict by setting up play situations in which the child

17

dramatized and displaced onto doll figures his feelings
about the various caretakers in his life. Original
story situations (See Appendix) required the child doll
to select various adult dolls to help in situations of
specific need.

A projective interview such as this assumes that
the child, in telling what the same sex doll will do,
expresses his own motives. Leon Yarrow believes that
this technique is particularly appropriate for children
between the ages of three and five, since the appeal and
"concreteness" of the dolls stimulate more communication
via symbolic play than would occur verbally.[1] According
to Piaget, the child who plays with dolls remakes his
own life as he would like it to be.[2]

A Questionnaire given to all seventy-five of the
regular caretakers of the children in this study sought
their opinions regarding the child's preference for
specific caretakers in the same situations as those presented in the doll play interview. Situations were
studied in which attachment responses most likely would
be evident. These include:

1. Separation and reunion experiences
2. Bed-time (Separation)
3. Dinner (Nurturance)
4. Free play
5. Fear situations (when the child is hurt or lost)

Mary Ainsworth, who worked with Bowlby and subsequently
has written extensively about the subject of attachment,
states:

> Attachment behavior is more likely
> to be activated if an infant is hun-
> gry, in pain, tired or ill than when
> he is rested, well fed, and healthy.
> Attachment behavior is likely to be
> activated, often at high intensity,
> when a child is alarmed, or when the
> attachment figure moves away, departs,
> or is absent—and especially if it is
> inexplicably and seemingly irretriev-
> ably lost. Other conditions include
> the return of an attachment figure
> after an absence, or rebuff either by
> that figure or someone else.[3]

18

The original stories created for this study contain themes deliberately intended to elicit attachment responses, based on Ainsworth's schema. The five story themes are: Hurt, Nurturance (Dinner), Bedtime, Fear/ Separation, and Play/Recreation.[4] In parallel fashion, the questionnaire contains questions about the child's preferences for specific caretakers in situations comparable to those covered by the stories. The combined use of these two techniques—the doll play interview with the children, and the caretaker questionnaire— tapped the opinions and feelings of each respectively regarding the significance of the other in situations which stimulate attachment responses.

Another approach to studying comples relationships is the direct observation by a specialist, who notes first-hand how people interact with each other. This method, Participant Observation, is

> Characterized by a period of in-
> tense social interaction between
> the researcher and the subjects, in
> the milieu of the latter. During
> this period, data are unobtrusively
> and systematically collected.[5]

This approach seemed tailor-made to detect information about relationships, which although obvious to an observer, might be unrecognized by the principals.[6] Kerlinger states that "important as is asking about behavior there is no substitute for seeing, as directly as possible, what people actually do when confronted with different circumstances and different people".[7]

Since the intent of the observations was to study the quality of the child's attachment relationships, the visiting schedule was set up to coincide with times when as previously indicated, attachment responses would most likely occur. This visiting schedule, discussed with the parents during the initial home visit, included:

1. a dinner observation
2. a bedtime observation
3. an observation when the parents were leaving the child with a baby sitter
4. a visit at the day care center which involved observation of the child with the teacher, as well as the child's reactions when the parent came to pick him up

5. observation of the child with at least
   one "regular" sitter

A total of six or seven separate observation visits
(including in addition to the list above, the Introductory Visit and a Play Sesssion with the child) occurred for each child and family in the study over a period
of several weeks. (See Table I.) The projective doll
play interview with the child occurred after the child
had become well acquainted with the researcher, based
on several visits in the child's home and in the day
care center.

These three techniques—structured doll play interviews with the child, caretaker questionnaires, and
naturalistic observations of the child in the course of
everyday routine activities—provided three different
vantage points for exploration of the topic of children's relationships with their various caretakers.
This multi-method approach, although time-consuming,
was appropriate and necessary to uncover the intri-
cacies, complexities, and varieties of the attachment
responses under study.

## Getting Started

Having determined the method for studying the
topic, we now needed to collate a core group of families
willing to participate in the research. It was essential to keep the sample size small, since the task of
studying the subtleties of relationships required repeated observations and the building of trust and
familiarity over time between the researcher and the
families. The goal of this study was to identify and
analyze the range and quality of each child's attachment relationships with his regular caretakers.

Any child enrolled in an all-day preschool program
is, by definition, receiving multiple caretaking. Day
care centers are, thus, logical settings in which to
find children suitable for a study of children's relationships with different caretakers. Locating the
children, however, is only the first step. Engaging
the interest and support of their busy working parents
is a separate challenge. Beginnings always require
ingenuity and careful planning. In this instance, cooperation of the day care directors was essential since
they function in the role of "gatekeepers," between the
families and the researcher.

| TABLE I |  |  |
| --- | --- | --- |
| SEQUENCE OF DATA COLLECTION |  |  |
| Situation | Place | Type of Data |
| Introductory Visit | Home | Observation Parent Questionnaires |
| Observation #1 | Day Care Center | Caretaker Questionnaire |
| Family Dinner | Home | Observation Projective(a) |
| Sitter #1 | Home or Sitter's Home | Observation Caretaker Questionnaire |
| Observation #2 | Day Care Center | Observation Teacher Questionnaire |
| Sitter #2 | Home or Sitter's Home | Observation Caretaker Questionnaire |
| Play Session | Day Care Center or Home | Projective(b) |
| Bed-time Visit | Home | Observation Caretaking History |

(a) Child was asked to Draw a Person and to Draw his Family.
(b) Child was asked to complete Five structured doll play stories.

Preliminary meetings with directors in three day care centers resulted in their agreement to send introductory letters to selected parents, inviting them to participate in a study of "typical behavior of four and five year old children." The researcher was introduced in the letters as a professional social worker currently completing her doctoral degree. The letter stressed the importance of the study as potentially adding to scientific knowledge about children. The parents were asked to return a tear sheet indicating their willingness to let the researcher call them.

The Centers. Geographic proximity to the researcher's home was a prime consideration in selecting centers since the study design required repeated observation visits with each child at different times of day and night.

Two of the three centers selected had the largest and second largest enrollments in the county,[8] among a total of nine all-day programs then in operation. Fourteen of the nineteen families who participated in the study came from these two centers. Cooperation of two other centers subsequently increased the total number of participating families.

## The Study Sample

Since the research plan involved an in-depth study of a small number of children, the strategy was to work with as homogeneous a group as possible. Focus on a small, homogeneous group offered the possibility of uncovering salient features about relationships which would be more evident in a clear-cut, standardized group than in a heterogeneous assortment of children and families.

Requirements for a representative random sample do not apply to a qualitative research approach such as this study. Illustrated in the detailed, repeated observations and intensive study method of Freud and Piaget, the qualitative approach to research strives for new theoretical understanding and insight in previously unexplored areas. This goal is more attainable by in-depth study of a small, discrete group.

The following considerations determined the selection of the small group of families who were solicited to participate in this study:

1. Intactness of the marriage
2. Race
3. Age of child
4. Length of time in day care

Intactness of the marriage was the first and primary criterion, based on the assumption that a child's relationship with one or both parents might be profoundly affected by the absence of one due to divorce, separation or death. Therefore, only children who were living with both parents were included in this study.

Since there were more children from intact white families in the three centers which initially agreed to cooperate with the researcher, race became the second criterion in drawing the sample. Although this was a decision which evolved from the parents' marital status, it also makes sense in terms of well documented differences in child rearing practices among different racial groups[9] which might have a significant impact on attachment formation and relationships.

Age was a third factor in the goal of a homogeneous sample. Since attachment relationships of "older" preschool children had not been studied previously, children between the ages of four and six became the focus for this research. This requirement was subsequently relaxed three months at the lower end in order to include two more children in the study. Five-year-olds were included only if they were not attending kindergarten. There were five five-year-olds in the final sample of nineteen.

Length of time in day care was an additional factor in obtaining the sample. Since the child's relationship with the day care teacher was one of the interactions to be studied, we wanted the child to be well integrated into the program and familiar with the teacher.

The requirement was set at three month's minimum enrollment in the center prior to the beginning of the research study. By far the majority of the children in the study had been enrolled for seven months or more, with only one child in the three month minimum category.

23

The working status of the mothers was not a pre-
determined criterion, in view of the assumption that
few parents would enroll their preschool children in
an all-day program unless they themselves were otherwise occupied. This proved to be correct in all but
two of the nineteen families. It was the two mothers
who were <u>not</u> working who subsequently withdrew from the
study, one because her husband was "never home," and
hence unavailable to participate, and the other, who
refused to complete the final visit after she began a
part-time job and said she was "too tired."

<u>Recruitment</u>. Letters inviting participation were sent
to thirty-seven parents, of whom nineteen responded
positively; seventeen became the final population
studied. The total enrollment of children aged four
and five in these five Centers was one hundred and
fifty. The fact that only thirty-seven invitational
letters were sent reflects the very high number of
single parent families whose children were enrolled
in these programs, in addition to children who did not
meet the study criteria in terms of race, length of
time enrolled, and age.


## The Participating Families

The truism about busy people getting a lot done
applies aptly to many of the families who participated
in this study. The portrayal of the daily grind of
Adam and Eve Armstrong also describes their parents.
These couples not only hold responsible jobs, sometimes
requiring up to an hour commute twice a day; they also
have to food shop, cook, do laundry, take children for
allergy shots, attend parent-teacher conferences, clean
the house, shovel snow, bathe the preschoolers, plan
birthday parties, arrange sitters for evenings out, en-
tertain relatives for family dinners on holidays, keep
up with the bill payments, toilet train the toddlers,
and occasionally, take "work" home from the office!
This is a short list of incredible responsibilities
which for several months in 1978 also included juggling
schedules to permit a social work researcher to come
into their homes for four or five one-to-two-hour-
visits "during everyday routine activities."

This may, in fact, have been an unusual group of
families, comfortable enough about their lives to let
a stranger get a glimpse of some very intimate moments.

24

The possibility of being "on their best behavior" wanes when young children are involved, since preschoolers who may have some sense of "company manners," will not maintain any pretense after familiarity sets in.

Motivation for Participation. A number of mothers and fathers in the study were themselves currently working on advanced degrees, or had recently finished school, and several mentioned their willingness to participate in the study because it involved goals they understood and valued. Two families had a remote connection with the researcher's university and this evidently had inspired their participation.

Often people volunteer to participate in a project when they anticipate some personal gain as an outcome. In this instance the researcher was alert for questions which suggested parental concerns about their children's development. This occurred in two instances. The mother of a temperamentally difficult boy (Matthew) asked in the last visit, "He's normal, isn't he?" and the mother of the youngest child in the study (Lori) asked in the third visit, "So what are you finding out about my girl?" These questions were answered directly, briefly and honestly, stressing the research emphasis on looking for a range of behavior, rather than on evaluation of any individual child.

The degree to which this group of families resembles or differs from "the average family" will never be known; they did open their doors and participate wholeheartedly in a project which sometimes required complicated coordination among their children's various caretakers.

The following section reviews the characteristics of the families in this study. The parents disclosed much information spontaneously during the course of the visits as the families gradually developed a trusting relationship with the researcher. During the final observation visit, the researcher asked questions about details of the parents' work history and the accompanying caretaking arrangements for the child, when this was not already known.

The Parents. The thirty-four individual parents (of the seventeen families which completed the study) ranged in age from twenty-two to fifty-six years, with thirty-three the mean age for both mothers and fathers.

25

It was the first marriage for all but two individuals.
The group was well educated, with all except one having
graduated from high school and most having completed
some years of college. Eight parents had master's degrees and one had a doctorate. Their occupations included four who had their own businesses, three who
were nurses, two landscapers, and five who were involved
in academia, either as teachers, professors, counselors
or administrators. Three were engineers, four were in
sales, and three were involved in accounting and financial analysis. One each worked as a secretary, podia-
trist, social worker, mechanic, public relations con-
sultant, artist, occupational therapist, and buyer.
One woman helped her husband in their shared business
and another was a student who also worked part-time in
her son's day care center as an aide.

Four mothers and two fathers were working on
advanced degrees in addition to their regular employment. This usually meant either Saturday, or evening,
classes with complicated baby-sitting arrangements to
compensate for their absences. The difficulty of finding time to study and write papers was mentioned by
several; however, none considered abandoning their edu-
cational goals to alleviate this pressure.

The Children. The seventeen study children ranged in
age from three years, nine months to five years, six
months, with the mean age four years, seven months.
Twelve of the children had siblings and five did not.
Among those who had siblings, eight had one and four
had two; eight were the youngest in their family, while
four were the oldest.

All of the children had been enrolled in their
current day care setting for at least three months,
since this was a precondition for participation. Most
had been enrolled for seven months or more, with only
one child in the minimum three month category. A total
of nine had been enrolled for seven, eight or nine
months, while seven had been enrolled fifteen months or
more.

There were eight girls in the study and nine boys,
with the girls having been enrolled in the centers approximately twice as long as had most of the boys.

Age of Child When Mother Returned to Work or School.
Families in which the mother works or goes to school

constituted the majority in this study population.
Only one mother of the seventeen was not currently working, and this was due to recent childbirth which had in-
terrupted a full time job as a teacher and student.
Although the researcher had expected to encounter a
majority of currently working mothers among the population of day care children, there was no way to anticipate the length of time the mother had been working.
The researcher anticipated a great deal of variation
in the mothers' work histories. In actuality, of the
seventeen study children, twelve mothers had returned
to full or part-time work or school during the first
year of the child's life. Another two returned by the
time the child was two years old, and only three of the
seventeen mothers waited until their child was thirty-
one months or older to return to work or school. See
Table II below for a summarized breakdown.

| TABLE II | | | |
|----------|---|---|---|
| SUMMARY OF STUDY CHILDREN'S AGES WHEN MOTHERS RETURNED TO FULL OR PART-TIME WORK OR SCHOOL | | | |
| Age of Child | Full Time | Part Time | Total |
| 0 - 6 Mos. | 3 | 5 | 8 |
| 7 - 12 Mos. | 3 | 1 | 4 |
| 13 - 18 Mos. | 1 | 0 | 1 |
| 19 - 24 Mos. | 0 | 1 | 1 |
| 25 - 30 Mos. | 0 | 0 | 0 |
| 31 - 37 Mos. | 2 | 0 | 2 |
| 38 - 44 Mos. | 0 | 1 | 1 |
| TOTAL | 9 | 8 | 17 |

The majority of the women had been working or in
school prior to the birth of the study child, and most
returned to the same or similar employment after a
maternity leave of absence. The advent of the child
was taken very much in stride by most. One mother
worked until the day before her child (Louis) was born;
two mothers were still nursing their children when they

returned to work, the children being seven months (Lori) and eight months (Jeff) respectively. One mother, (Ronald's) stated that she never stopped working when Ronald was born—she claims that she took work to the hospital with her, and that subsequently she was able to bring the baby with her to work, which proceeded without interruption (and, it would seem, without a mother-child separation, due to a unique employment situation). The other extreme is Matthew's mother who began working as an aid in the day care center simultaneous with his enrollment there at age three and a half, and Cindy's mother who waited until the child was three before enrolling in a college nursing program. The type of caretaking provided for the children varied greatly and will be discussed in detail in Chapter 4.

## NOTES

1. Yarrow, Leon, "Interviewing Children," in Paul Mussen, ed., <u>Handbook of Research Methods in Child Development</u> (New York: John Wiley & Sons) 1960, pp. 585-590.

2. Piaget, Jean, <u>Six Psychological Studies</u>, David Elkind, ed. (New York: Vintage) 1968, p. 17.

3. Ainsworth, Mary, "Attachment Theory and Its Utility in Cross-Cultural Research" in <u>Culture and Infancy: Variations in the Human Experience</u>, P. H. Leiderman, ed. (New York: Academic) 1977, p. 53.

4. Leon Yarrow suggested in a personal interview with the author in December 1977 that a child's choice for proximity and contact when all his other needs have been met is a possible indicator of attachment preference. Hence the story theme with the play element. An article by Daniel Stern, "The goal and structure of mother-infant play" in <u>Journal of the American Academy of Child Psychiatry</u>, (1974, 13, pp. 402-421) discusses the importance of infant-mother play in the attachment relationship.

5. Bogdan, Robert, and Taylor, Steven, <u>Introduction to Qualitative Research Methods</u> (New York: John Wiley & Sons) 1975, p. 5.

6. See Morris Zelditch, "Some Methodological Problems
   of Field Studies" in George McCall and J. L. Simmons,
   Issues in Participant Observation (Reading, Mass.:
   Addison-Wesley Publishing Co.) 1969, p. 18. Zelditch
   refers to the great value of participant observation
   in detecting latent phenomena; observable events of
   which the subjects may be unaware, but which can be
   directly apprehended by the observer.

7. Kerlinger, Fred, Foundations of Behavioral Research,
   2nd ed. (New York: Holt, Rinehart and Winston, Inc.)
   1973, p. 554.

8. Since the researcher promised confidentiality to the
   families who participated, no identifying names are
   used in this report. The County from which the population is drawn is located within a twenty-mile
   radius of New York City. Population is approximately
   900,000, distributed over an area of more than two
   hundred square miles.

9. See, for example, Carol Stack, All Our Kin (New York:
   Harper and Row) 1974. We do not know about the impact on attachment relationships of the practices of
   "child-keeping" and routine and extensive involvement
   of the extended family in child care, some of which
   may involve lengthy periods of separation of the
   child from the parents.

# II  CARETAKING NETWORKS

## II  CARETAKING NETWORKS

Young children of working parents depend on a network of caretakers to assume the protective and socialization functions traditionally provided by the mother alone. The caretaking network may be large or small, and the mesh of intersecting responsibilities may be coarse or fine, but ultimately every thread in the pattern is critical.

The research reported here focuses on the child's relationships with their caretakers, who were responsible for the child's routine care at least three hours per week, over a period of at least three month's duration. Recent, or sporadic caretaking contacts were not studied. Although many children receive extensive ad hoc care beyond the regular arrangements established in conjunction with their parents' work, they usually do not establish meaningful bonds with these intermittent caretakers. Sometimes parents "trade" informal caretaking responsibilities among neighbors, friends and relatives for reasons of economy and convenience. These extemporaneous, sporadic arrangements significantly extend each child's network of caretakers, and add to the child's repertoire of life experience with different caretaking adults. However, it is most unlikely that the child would form attachment bonds with caretakers known only intermittently and casually in this fashion.

Although we did not label or diagnose the families who participated in the study, it nonetheless became evident that some families were involved with a broad network of relatives, friends and regular caretakers, while other families cast their nets infrequently and did not involve non-related caretakers in their child's routine care. Minuchin's concepts of "enmeshed" and "disengaged" family styles[1] seem to apply to patterns of child care, in addition to characterizing the family's social relationships in general. These concepts convey the extent to which the family actively seeks interactions beyond its own members.

Financial considerations sometimes override the family's preferences in regard to child care, since grandmother is usually cheaper than a hired sitter, and sometimes even when the family would prefer the sitter, grandmother ends up with the job. Conversely,

when grandmother is working or unavailable to help,
families which might prefer care by a relative end up
making arrangements with an unrelated sitter. Obviously
the range and continuity of the child's experience with
other people determines the scope of attachment options
available to him.

Chapter 3 discusses the meaning of the day care
experience to the child in terms of providing potentially enriching opportunities for relationships with teachers and peers. Chapter 4 identifies and describes the
five forms of caretaking used by the families in this
study, in addition to day care. These five caretaking
patterns, plus day care or other preschool program,
constitute the major child care alternatives available
to all families, whether the parents work or not.

NOTES

1. Minuchin, Salvatore, et. al., <u>Families of the Slums</u>
   (New York: Basic Books) 1969, pp. 352-358.

## Chapter Three

## THE COMMON DENOMINATOR OF DAY CARE

Hundreds of thousands of preschoolers, like the children in this study, live in at least two differnt worlds—that of their own family, and that of the day care center, where they spend the bulk of their waking hours.  Gesell and Ilg describe the typical four-year-old as a "truly social being who wants to be with playmates,"[1] and the typical five-year-old as "ripe for enlarged community experience."[2]  Thus, the day care setting facilitates group involvement and peer relationships at a time when the developmental thrust of the four and five-year-old child is reaching for just such social contacts.

The day-long group experience of day care, five days a week was a commonality for all the children in this study, whether they had one, or a half-a-dozen other regular caretakers during evening and weekend hours.  All children spent an average of forty hours per week with the same group of peers, in the care of a regular "teacher" and an assortment of "aides."  The routine of these centers included periods of indoor and outdoor play, mid-morning and mid-afternoon snacks, a hot lunch at noon followed by a rest period on individual cots, and periodic special trips to the library, the fire house, the zoo and other local attractions.

Variations among the centers, as in any school or human service facility, reflected the personalities, training and commitment of individual staff members. We were impressed, for example, with the difference in noise level in centers which had roughly the same enrollment.  Repeated observations of teacher-child interactions suggested that the children were quieter and more involved in their own activities in the center where the teachers periodically gave individual children one-to-one attention, as compared to the "noisy" center where the teachers attempted more group interaction and instruction, and often ended up raising their voices themselves in order to be heard.

Individual family schedules led to other differences in the day care experience for individual children.  Some children, like Adam Armstrong, arrived at their centers by 8:00 a.m.; many of the early arrivals had breakfast there.  Other children arrived later, depending on their parents' work schedule.  The end of the day also presented a diverse picture in terms of who picked the child up and at what time. Several centers planned the afternoon free play activity period outdoors from 4-5:00 p.m. to accomodate the parents and sitters who arrived sequentially, and plucked their charges from the playing group. One center had van transportation at the end of the day for children whose caretakers could not pick them up. None of the centers in this study could care for a child beyond 6:00 p.m. so children whose parents were not home from work by then needed to arrange supplemental care.

About half (eight of the seventeen study children) received regular, non-parental care during the three-month period of the research study. This was provided by non-relatives in six instances. The fact that ten of the study children did not receive any regular care beyond day care and parental care during this period stands in sharp contrast to the rather erratic pattern of care which in many instances had preceded the children's entry into the full day program. Day care, for the four and five-year-old children in this study provided continuity and stability both in routine and in caretakers.

Relationships With Day Care Teachers. Ask any kindergarten or first grade teacher how many times a day they are called "Mommy," and the significance of the day care teacher as mother substitute becomes evident. For the three to five-year-old child, the day care teacher plays many roles, most of which, in other circumstances, would have been performed by the child's mother. These multiple functions include giving support, praise, instruction, discipline, protection, food, rest, and stimulation.

A major difference in day care as compared to most home environments is that the day care teacher is responsible for a group of six to twelve children at one time, all of whom need her involvement in all of these different ways. Some children in this study were more successful in having their needs met by their teachers than were others. This fact seemed related to the child's temperament in addition to the "goodness-of-fit" between the child's basic behavioral style and that of the teacher. Since consideration of the child's temperament is vital in understanding the teacher-child relationship, this will be discussed prior to giving illustrations of teacher-child interaction which demonstrate the distinct temperamental variables.

<u>Child's Intrinsic Interactive Style</u>.  Children, like
adults, have different, but consistent ways of relating
to other people.  We noticed that some children in this
study were very outgoing, social and direct in their
manner, while others were shy, self-contained and sometimes uninvolved.  A few were oppositional, persistent,
and sometimes aggressively dominant and assertive in
their general style of relating.

We categorized the "intrinsic interactive style"
of each child according to three broad groups:

1. The outgoing, social and verbal child
2. The shy, self-contained, and sometimes
   uninvolved child
3. The oppositional, persistent, and sometimes aggressive and dominant child

Our categorization, independently derived, corresponds
strikingly with Thomas and Chess' three basic temperamental constellations which they derived from a twenty-
year longitudinal study of one hundred thirty-six individual children from eighty families.  Thomas and Chess'
basic temperamental types are as follows:

> The <u>Difficult Child</u> reacts strongly
> and negatively to new situations,
> adapts slowly and is irregular in
> his eating and sleeping habits.
> Totally different is the <u>Easy Child</u>
> who has regular habits and adapts
> quickly to new experiences, with
> positive expression of mood.  The
> <u>Slow-To-Warm-Up Child</u> approaches
> new situations with hesitancy but
> without strong negative reactions,
> and adapts positively if not pres-
> sured.[3]

The present research did not seek extensive
<u>detailed</u> information regarding the regularity of the
child's sleeping, eating and other habits on which to
make the definitive temperamental assessments of Thomas
and Chess.  It is, nonetheless, evident that our three
types of "intrinsic interactive style" are analogous to
Thomas and Chess' three basic temperamental constellations.  In other words, our first category—the outgoing, social and verbal child is similar to Thomas and

Chess' _Easy Child_; our second category—the shy, self-contained and sometimes uninvolved child is comparable to Thomas and Chess' _Slow-To-Warm-Up Child_; and our third group—the oppositional, persistent and sometimes aggressive and dominant child falls into Thomas and Chess' _Difficult Child_ category.

Our assessment of the study children's "Intrrinsic Interactive Style" (See Table III) was based on six or seven hours of observation of each child with different people in different situations. We considered the categories as _general_ approximations of the child's style, with no child one hundred percent consistent in his manner of relating. However, we believe that these interactive styles are _very_ distinctive, especially the "Easy" and the "Difficult" categories. The "Slow-To-Warm" we view as an _initial_ mode of response, beyond which the child can often be further categorized into "Easy" or "Difficult."

The _consistency of the child's behavior across settings_ was impressive and led to our appreciation of the considerable _impact of the child's temperament and personality on the significant people in his environment_. For example, the very verbal child (e.g., Elizabeth) chatted, questioned and typically received a great deal of enthusiastic verbal interchange at home, at school and at her sitter's house, while the very labile child (e.g., Lori) pouted, cried and whined wherever she went, frequently producing an irritated response from others.

This finding of the overriding influence of the child's temperament on different caretakers across various settings suggests that the narcissistic young child does not readily adapt to the world around him. Caretakers therefore should consider the child's basic temperamental style in order to avoid conflict. An example follows of a difficult child who was a "handful" for any adult interacting with her. The teacher in this instance did not become irritated with the child, and helped the child develop more effective peer relationships.

```
┌─────────────────────────────────────────────────────────────┐
│                        TABLE III                            │
│                                                             │
│     "INTRINSIC INTERACTIVE STYLES" OF STUDY CHILDREN        │
│            AS RELATED TO THOMAS AND CHESS'                   │
│          THREE TEMPERAMENTAL CONSTELLATIONS*                │
├─────────────────────────────────────────────────────────────┤
```

I. Interactive Style:  Social, Outgoing, Verbal
   Temperamental Constellation:  Easy Child

              Annalee              Ronald
              Nina                 Scott
              Elizabeth            Steven
              John                 Diane


II. Interactive Style:  Shy, Self-Contained, Some-
                        times Uninvolved
    Temperamental Constellation:  Slow-To-Warm-Up Child

              Cindy                Louis
              Kathy                James
              Donald               Paul


III. Interactive Style:  Oppositional, Persistent, Some-
                         times Aggressive and Dominant
     Temperamental Constellation:  Difficult Child

              Lori                 Matthew
              Kim                  Walter
              Linda


     ─────────────────────────

     *Alexander Thomas and Stella Chess, Temperament
     and Development (New York: Brunner/Mazel, 1977)
     p-. 22-23.

Interactive Style: Oppositional, Persistent,
Sometimes Aggressive and
Dominant
Temperamental Constellation: "Difficult" Child
Child's Name:       Kim

Interaction with Peers and Teacher
    (C=Child; T=Teacher)
Day Care Observation:   Outdoor Free Play
Activity

Children were climbing up and down a ladder
which gave access to an elevated play house.
C said to another child: "You get off there
or I'll smack your face." C pushed the child
down and ran away. T went up to C and made
her come back to the child she had pushed.
T to C: "If you're angry you tell her, don't
push her." T began working with both children in setting up the play area again.

Later: C continued to try to prevent certain children from playing in a certain
area (her territory?). After returning to
the area and noticing a child on the ladder,
C said: "Tara get off. I'm going to throw
this ball on your pee-pee." Tara left.
Another child came over. C said: "Tyrone,
no! You get out of here. This ball is
going to go on you."

Later: Inside—after outdoor play activity.
Children were using the bathroom and preparing to begin an art activity. C to T: "I
want to wash the table." T gave C a cloth
to do so and C ran to the sink to wet it.
C began wiping the table with much energy.
C appeared angry with one child who was
sitting with her elbows on the table. She
pushed the child's elbows off the table so
she could wipe underneath them. C noticed
that the other child had a runny nose.
C to child: "Your face is disgusting!"
T to C: "Get him a tissue."
C to T: "He's the one who needs a tissue."
T to C: "Get him a tissue, Kim.
C got the tissue and gave it to the child.

Comment: This child seems to have an angry, aggressive mode of interacting with her peers. She dominates and intimidates them. The teacher is firm and direct with her and maintains control.

Additional examples of children's temperamental styles will be given in the discussion of relationships with other caretakers.

Teachers as Attachment Figures. When does a caretaker, such as a teacher, become an object of attachment for the young child, and how do we know that such a special relationship exists? Our previous discussion of attachment defined it as a relationship signifying special bonds of affection to specific people. It is logical to assume that the day care teacher could become a very significant person in the child's life, considering the important, multi-faceted roles the mother-substitute-teacher plays for the child.

Attachments of babies and young children have been studied by observing the toddler's protest when the mother goes away, and the child's tendency to remain close to her when she returns.[4] Thus, separation anxiety is considered an indication that attachment has occurred. Schaffer states:

> When the physical proximity of a
> particular individual is sought
> in its own right an attachment
> may be said to have been formed
> to that particular individual,
> and to test for this occurrence
> one may best observe the child's
> behavior in conditions where he
> is prevented from attaining such
> proximity.[5]

The more highly developed cognitive ability and communication skills of the older preschool child protect him from the fear that proximity is essential for an enduring relationship. Awareness of object constancy allows the older preschooler to tolerate separations without assuming that the loved person no longer exists when she leaves the room. The fact that the three-year-old child no longer expresses the same separation protest of baby and toddlerhood must not be taken as an indication that the attachment bond itself is

41

weakened, however. Bowlby states that "most children after their third birthday show attachment behavior less urgently and frequently than before; it nonetheless still constitutes a major part of behavior."[6]

Two spontaneously reported instances of grieving on the part of two study children over their separation from a day care teacher indicated that these children had each become "attached" to their teachers, and had considerable difficulty relinquishing these relationships, and reattaching to subsequent teachers.

Example A: James had experienced little multiple caretaking prior to his mother's decision to enroll him in day care at age three so that she could attend college. James was in the same center and remained with the same teacher for two years, whereupon his mother transferred him to another center closer to her then current job. James resisted becoming involved in the new center and repeatedly asked his mother why he couldn't return to his former center and to his former teacher. The teacher in the new center told the researcher about the great difficulty she had in involving James in the program when he first entered.

Example B: Ronald had experienced many extremes of caretaking in his four years. After his birth his mother kept him with her in a basket for several months as she actively continued her job as a religious education director in the school across the street from the family's home. When Ronald was eighteen months old his twin brothers were born, and the family employed and fired a virtual flock of babysitters, most of whom were unable to manage the responsibilities of the three young children. At age three, Ronald entered day care and formed a very close attachment to his teacher.

According to Ronald's parents, the child's feeling was reciprocated by the teacher who treated him as her "pet." In this cen-

ter, as in many, there was a mandatory
shift of teachers at the point the children moved from the "three-year-old" to
the "four-year-old" group, even though
many of the core group of children remained the same. In this instance the expectation was that the four-year-olds "gradu-
ate" to the classroom upstairs. Ronald's
mother recalls that for several weeks he
would literally attach himself and cling
to his former teacher when he arrived in
the morning, and have to be pried loose
and carried upstairs screaming and kick-
ing all the way. The parents believe that
Ronald still feels a very "special bond"
to this teacher, and that he never really
accepted the transfer.

This last example is a dramatic instance of the un-
fortunate disregard of a child's attachment to a teacher.
The frequent practice of changing teachers of three,
four and five-year-old children in day care should be
evaluated in terms of the meaning this has for children
who may have developed attachments to their teachers.
Although most children tolerate the change, it might be
argued that a two-year period with the same teacher
would promote healthy attachment formation without risk-
ing possible detrimental trauma for children, like
Ronald, who find the transfer painful.

Relationship with Peers. Although the present research
did not investigate the existence and nature of friendship bonds between children in day care, there were several instances in which such friendships stood out as
especially significant. Many children remain in the
same center with a nucleus of the same peer group for
several years. Their contacts with each other often
develop a sibling-like quality, with the complex over-
tones of competiveness and affection this relationship
implies.

Some children go to one another's homes to have
dinner, to play on weekends, and occasionally, to stay
for the night. As often happens with school-age children, the friendships of the children may instigate
contact and friendships among the parents. This was
very apparent with two study children (Linda and Nina)
whose teacher indicated that "they always do everything
together, including participation in a research study!"

Recent studies have challenged previous beliefs that preschoolers are not socially capable of developing "real" friendships.[7]  After a year observing three-year-olds at a nursery school in California, Zick Rubin concluded that:

> some preschoolers have relationships
> that are strikingly reminiscent of
> the attachment of adult spouses, or
> the camaraderie of adult co-workers,
> or even between those of adult men-
> tors and their proteges.[8]

An article in <u>Orthopsychiatry</u> (April 1981) approaches the topic of peer interaction from the perspective of spontaneous "peer psychotherapy" in a day care setting, in which a youngster facilitated the socialization of a withdrawn, older peer.[9]  The contribution of age-mate play to normal development, recognized initially by primate researchers,[12] now is considered equally important for humans, according to the Ortho article.

Friendships among the study children were most frequent among the group of children we categorized as "Social, Outgoing and Verbal."  Impressive mutuality and enjoyment often occurred in their fantasy stories, overheard and recorded during the day care observations:

<u>Example</u>:  Steven and Diane
<u>Day Care Observation</u>:  Indoors

The children were seated next to each other at a table, each engaged in assembling separate jigsaw puzzles.  Steven initiated the following conversation which was about his brother, Jack, two years older:

S to D:  "I'm going to scream in Jack's
          ear, then he'll run in the
          street, and a truck will run
          over him and he'll be flat as
          a pancake."
D to S:  "Then we'll cut him up."
S to D:  "No. We'll roll him up and make
          him into a carpet."
D to S:  "For me!"
S to D:  "No. For me.  My Jack carpet!"
Both children laughed hilariously.

The desire of the young child to gain dominance
and control often gets expressed in play, either verbally, as in the previous example, or behaviorally, as in
the following:

Example: Louis and Gail
Home Observation: Outside

Father and Louis' older sister were taking
care of him, while Mother was out. It was
a Saturday and Gail, a friend from the center, had come for lunch. Gail planned to
spend the afternoon playing at Louis' house.
L and G began swinging on the swing set.
F who was doing yard work, came over to
adjust the swing heights.
L to F: "I want mine higher than G's."
L and G began swinging. F returned to
trimming bushes at the corner of the
house. Gail got off the swing and went
up a low ladder attached to a slide. It
was wet at the bottom and L knew it, since
he had stood at the bottom feeling it. L
went up behind G and pushed her down.
L to G: "You're going to get a wet heine."
F came over.
F to L: "Why did you do that? Now she's
         all wet."
L went over to the swing and was smiling.
G ran and sat on the swing L had been using.
L whined and told G to get off. G ignored
him.
L ran toward the house. When G saw L leaving, she said she'd get off.

Comment: Louis' rather aggressive, dominant
play may be one of the few areas in his life
where he can assert himself definitively.
Louis has two teen-age sisters, who treat him
very much like the "baby brother" he is, sometimes indulging him, but always giving him
directions. Play, thus, provides Louis with
a chance to gain mastery over someone else, an
experience which unfortunately puts the other
child in a very subordinate position. Prior
to playing outdoors, Louis and Gail ate their
lunches on trays in the den, and seemed to
be quite happy together.

45

Sociability and friendship pairs were by no means universal among the children in this study, but the strength and persistance of some unions was most impressive. Steven and Diane were one such pair, as were Linda and Nina.

<u>Example</u>: Linda
<u>Family Dinner Observation</u>

This was a conversation between Linda and her mother about Linda's friendship with Nina.

M to L: "Nina taught you a lot of things, didn't she? Didn't she teach you how to tie your shoes?"

L to M: "No. Mary taught me how to tie. Nina taught me how to spell LOVE."

Play and friendships with peers serve different purposes for only children and children with siblings. Steven's and Ronald's play suggest strong sibling rivalry, and their attempts to master this, wheras only children, such as Diane and Nina, gain through peer contacts important socialization experiences.

While it is doubtful that friendships such as these could accurately be termed "attachments," they are strong bonds, and serve an important purpose for the child.

A footnote on Linda and Nina's friendship occurred several months after the completion of the study when Linda's mother called the researcher saying that Linda had just come across the farewell book-gift the researcher had given her, which reminded them both of our visits and prompted them to call, "just to say Hello." The conversation revealed that Linda and Nina, who were currently attending kindergartens in separate towns, continue to see one another periodically, although "their relationship was not as close as it had been during the two years in day care."

<u>Links Between Home and Day Care</u>. The child's cyclical orbit between the two worlds of home and day care includes a lot of shuffling of objects and sharing of information back and forth between the two settings. On the one hand, art work and baked goodies travel home to be admired and sampled, while in the other direction new toys and special personal possessions accompany the

returning child who enjoys the status and attention these unique belongings confer on him in the group. Some children carry their "transitional objects"— blankets, teddy bears, etc.—with them on every trip back and forth. Many have baskets or satchels to accommodate their sweaters and various accumulations which require twice daily transport. Occasionally medicine and instructions go back and forth for the child who has recovered enough from an illness to return to group care, yet needs continuing medication several times a day. Most children have their own pillow and a sheet or cover from home which is distinctively theirs, which remains at the center for use at nap time. Some centers display photos of the child with various family members in locations visible and accessible for the children's examination and discussion.

Children's conversations naturally and spontaneously link the two worlds. For example, Elizabeth tells her teacher after painting a picture, "Hang it up so my Mommy can see it when she comes," and Kathy, "playing school" at home with a friend says, "I'm Miss Sally" (name of her teacher).

Children's behavior also reflects the mutual, interacting influence of their dual spheres. John's mother mentioned that he wanted to have his back rubbed every night because his teacher does it at school to help him go to sleep at nap time. Influences from home also reverberate in the day care setting sometimes in ways that can be very beneficial to the child. The following example illustrates a child's strong desire for physical proximity with her teacher. This observation occurred during a time when the child's mother was temporarily less available to her because of recent childbirth plus responsibility for a terminally ill mother-in-law.

Example: Kathy
Interaction With Teacher

K was working on a puzzle, sitting at a
table together with four or five other
children, all of whom were engaged in simi-
lar "board" activities.
T came over and stood by the table.
T to group: "How're you all doing?"
K to T: "I need help."
T sat down next to K and picked up a puzzle

piece, saying to K:  "What part does this
look like, Kathy?"
K moved over very close to T, and as she
did so T let her stand up at the table
between her legs.  T and K worked on the
puzzle together for a few minutes during
which time T lifted K to her lap.  Another
child came over and asked T for help and
T suggested to K that she could probably
finish the rest of the puzzle alone now.
T began helping the other child and K
finished the puzzle.
K to T:  "Look, Miss Sally."
T to K:  "Very good!"
K returned the puzzle to the shelf and
came back to the table with another one.
T noticed and said to K:  "Another one?"
The previous events were then repeated
with K ending up sitting on T's lap again.

Comment:  It was fascinating to observe the
playing out of the proximity seeking between
child and teacher.  We never saw Kathy's
teacher hold another child on her lap, in
more than a dozen hours of observations
at that center.  Kathy's quiet but quite
evident and persistent desire for physical
proximity suggests the presence of an attachment bond which this teacher consistently reciprocated.

There were many situations in which caretaker-
child interactions at home and school duplicated,
rather than complimented each other.  This similarity
of interactions across settings reflected the overriding influence of the child's temperament on caretakers,
as previously discussed.  Seeing Walter being coaxed to
drink his orange juice in school in a similar manner in
which his mother coaxed him to finish his dinner at home,
and seeing Kim's feisty aggressiveness at day care and
at home with her mother added a dimension of validity
to the observations in both settings, in addition to
emphasizing thepower of the child's temperament on interactions with various caretakers.

Teachers and parents both reciprocate and reinforce
the influence of one another on the developing young
child.  This shared responsibility flourishes when

values are compatible, communication links are open, and the goal of fostering the child's maximum development is paramount.


## NOTES

1. Gesell, Arnold and Ilg, Frances, <u>Child Development</u> (New York: Harper Bros.) 1949, p. 233.

2. Ibid., p. 249.

3. Thomas, Alexander and Chess, Stella, <u>Temperament and Development</u> (New York: Brunner/Mazel Publishers) 1977, jacket cover.

4. See, Mary Ainsworth and B Wittig, "Attachment and Exploratory Behavior of One-year-olds in a Strange Situation," in <u>Determinants of Infant Behavior IV.</u> ed. B. Foss (New York: Wiley) 1969.

   Separation protest and stranger anxiety are the basis for Mary Ainsworth's "Strange Situation," a standardized, twenty-one minute episode involving two brief planned separations from the mother, and three component three-minute segments with an adult female stranger present. The situation lends itself to coding in many different ways and has been used to interpret the existence and character of the child's attachment at different ages. Ainsworth designed the procedure for use with one-year-olds and she stated in a personal communication that she does not believe her Strange Situation is appropriate for use with children older than age two. This is because stranger anxiety and separation protest tend to diminish after this age. Variants of the Strange Situation have been used, however, with children up to age three, with two studies confirming decreased separation protest and stranger anxiety among older children.

5. Schaffer, Rudolph, "Some Issues for Research in the Study of Attachment Behavior," in <u>Determinants of Infant Behavior, II,</u> ed. B. Foss (New York: Wiley) 1968, p. 181.

6. Bowlby, _Attachment_, p. 254.

7. Collins, Glenn, "Friendship: A Fact of Life for Toddlers, Too," _The New York Times_, December 15, 1980.

8. See, for example, Rubin, Zick, _Children's Friendships_ (Cambridge, Mass.: Harvard University Press) 1980.

9. Mehl, Lewis E. and Peterson, Gail H., "Spontaneous Peer Psychotherapy in a Day Care Setting: A Case Report," _American Journal of Orthopsychiatry_, 51:2, April 1981, pp. 346-350.

10. Harlow, Harry and M. K., "Learning to Love," _American Scientist_, 54, 1966, pp. 244-272.

Chapter Four

CARETAKING PATTERNS: THE INNER CIRCLE AND BEYOND

Who is going to mind the baby while mother works or attends school?

Whereas fathers, grandmothers and hired sitters often assume some caretaking responsibilities even when mothers do not work outside the home, alternative arrangements are <u>mandatory</u> and must be specific when mothers have regular employment.

Families weigh a host of variables in the process of deciding how to apportion the care of their pre-school children. The following factors influenced the decisions of the families in this study:

- The mother's working hours
- The father's working hours
- Proximity, availability and willing-ness of relatives to help
- The family's financial resources for employing hired sitters, or arrang-ing group care
- The parents' values regarding non-familial caretakers
- Availability of suitable day care and/or hired sitters
- The age of the child

Every family tries to make an arrangement which they feel is best suited to their child and their own over-all convenience. Changes in the child-caring plan may occur often as time passes and the family's situation alters. Group care becomes popular after the child reaches age three, the traditional age for initiating preschool group experience.

The following section describes the various care-taking patterns utilized by the families in this study, beginning with a consideration of the age of the child and the arrangements for care when the mother returned to work or school. (See Table IV )

<u>Caretaking Histories Prior to Entry Into Day Care</u>
Since fourteen of the study children's mothers had re-turned to work or school by the time their children were two years old, alternative child care arrangements

were essential, especially for the seven whose mothers
worked full time. Some mothers arranged care in their
own homes, others took the child to a relative's, sitter's or family day care home, and in three families
the mother and father were able to stagger their work
schedules so that one or the other could be home with
the child. Table IV shows the breakdown of the children's ages when the mothers returned to full or part-
time work or school and the type of caretaking provided
at that time.

TABLE IV (a)

AGE OF CHILD
WHEN MOTHER RETURNED TO WORK OR SCHOOL
AND TYPE OF CARETAKING PROVIDED AT THAT TIME

| Names of Girls | Age of Child When Mother Returned To Work | Number of Hours Mother Worked/Week | Caretaking In Child's Or Sitter's Home |
|---|---|---|---|
| Lori | 7 mos. | 40 (eves) | C |
| Elizabeth | 2 mos. | 24 (days) | C |
| Kim | 2 mos. | 20 (eves) | C |
| Cindy | 36 mos. | 40 (days) | D.C. |
| Linda | 10 mos. | 20 (days) | C |
| Kathy | 18 mos. | 40 (days) | S |
| Annalee | 3 mos. | 40 (days) | S |
| Nina | 24 mos. | 20 (days) | S |

KEY:  D.C. = Day Care Center
        C = Child
        S = Sitter

      (a) = Girls
      (b) = Boys

52

## TABLE IV[b]

### AGE OF CHILD
### WHEN MOTHER RETURNED TO WORK OR SCHOOL
### AND TYPE OF CARETAKING PROVIDED AT THAT TIME

| Names of Boys | Age of Child When Mother Returned To Work | Number of Hours Mother Worked/Week | Caretaking In Child's Or Sitter's Home |
|---|---|---|---|
| Louis | 5 mos. | 35 (days) | S |
| Paul | 5 mos. | 20 (days) | S & C |
| Steven | 8 mos. | 40 (eves) | S & C |
| Ronald | 1 day | 40 (days) | C |
| James | 35 mos. | 40 (days) | D.C. |
| Scott | 6 mos. | 25 (days) | C |
| Walter | 6 mos. | 20 (eves & weekends) | C |
| John | 9 mos. | 40 (days) | S |
| Matthew | 42 mos. | 9 (days) | D.C. |

```
KEY:  D.C. = Day Care Center
         C  = Child
         S  = Sitter

        (a) = Girls
        (b) = Boys
```

As would be expected, there were many changes in these initial plans. Ten of the children experienced from one to three regular, non-parental caretakers prior to entry into day care, and five had been enrolled in half-day programs prior to entry into the current full-day program. Two children (James and Ronald) had had such an assortment of sitters the

53

parents could recall neither the precise number nor the circumstances of their turn over. Table V shows the breakdown of non-parental caretakers prior to day care entry.

| TABLE V | | | | | |
|---|---|---|---|---|---|
| NUMBER OF DIFFERENT, REGULAR, NON-PARENTAL CARETAKERS UTILIZED FOR STUDY CHILDREN PRIOR TO DAY CARE ENROLLMENT | | | | | |
| None | One | Two | Three | Four | Half-Day Nursery Programs |
| Scott | Cindy Kathy Nina | Louis Steven Lori Elizabeth | Paul Kim Linda | Annalee John | Matthew Walter Lori Paul Linda |

<u>Unique</u>

James - entered directly into day care, then had a variety of teen-age sitters.

Ronald - "had twenty-eight sitters in one year"—three boys under age two were difficult for most sitters; Ronald's twin brothers are eighteen months younger than he

Lori's experience illustrates the varied caretaking experience of the youngest child in this study (3 years, 9 months). Lori's caretaking history included contact with two different regular caretakers and one other day care program (for six weeks) prior to enrollment in the day care center at age three. For the last year Lori had been cared for every Saturday by a sitter while her parents worked in their store and she also had a regular sitter one night a week when her parents bowled.

Lori is one of the few study children who did not receive regular care from a relative (other than her parents). She had also been subjected to a turn over of routine baby-sitters. A live-in-housekeeper took care of her for about six months when she was between two and two-and-a-half, but the parents abruptly dismissed the woman when they began to suspect that she was unduly harsh in her discipline.

The section which follows gives details and examples of distinctive caretaking patterns utilized by working parents.

Five Patterns of Care. The families in this study utilized five distinct modes of caretaking in addition to day care for their children. The types of care are as follows:

1. Shared Parenting: This describes a division of caretaking in which both the mother and father are actively involved with child care tasks and responsibilities. In families which follow this pattern, the mother and father arrange their work schedule outside the home so that each is available to provide child care at home when the spouse is away, and vice versa. Sitters other than the parents are utilized only occasionally in this model, and not on a routine basis. Three of the families in this study fell into this category.

2. Mother/Father plus Relatives: Two of the study families followed this pattern. It involves caretaking on a regular basis provided by relatives in addition to care given by the parents. A grandmother was the relative in both instances in this study.

3. **Mother/Father plus Hired Sitters:** This was the model followed by five of the study families in which relatives were unavailable to provide caretaking. As with the other caretaking categories, it implies a planned caretaking arrangement on a regular basis.

4. **Mother/Father plus Relatives plus Hired Sitters:** This all-inclusive category was the pattern utilized by seven of the study families. It is the model providing for the most flexibility and variation, and thereby exposes the child to the widest range of caretaking experience.

5. **Mixed** (any of the above patterns) **with Minimal Involvement of Father:** The primary characteristic of this model is that the father does not involve himself with routine child caring activities. It occurred in each of the patterns described above and was characteristic of a total of seven of the study families.

Table VI indicates the specific caretaking patterns utilized by the study families.

Shared Parenting. The three families in which Shared Parenting was the primary model all were involved with relatives to a considerable extent, and two of these families probably would have utilized them for regular caretaking if geographic proximity had permitted. Two of the three mothers in the study who were nurses fall into this category, and both of their husbands own and manage their own businesses. This combination in the parents' occupations seemed to lend itself well to arranging work schedules so that one parent or the other was available to provide child care. The disadvantage for parents who work staggered shifts is the relatively little time they have together.

The willingness of fathers to participate actively in child care is as critical as is a flexible work schedule for the success of Shared Parenting.

```
                        TABLE   VI

              CARETAKING PATTERNS UTILIZED
                BY THE STUDY FAMILIES
```

|   TYPE OF PATTERN | NAME OF CHILD |
|---|---|
| 1. <u>Shared Parenting</u> | *Kim<br>Cindy<br>Scott |
| 2. <u>Mother/Father plus Relatives</u> | *Walter<br>*Nina |
| 3. <u>Mother/Father plus Unrelated<br>Sitters</u> | Lori<br>Elizabeth<br>*Annalee<br>Linda<br>Kathy |
| 4. <u>Mother/Father plus Relatives<br>plus Unrelated Sitters</u> | *John<br>*Matthew<br>*Louis<br>Ronald<br>Paul<br>James<br>Steven |
| 5.<u>*Mixed, with Minimal Involvement<br>of Father</u> | |

Scott's parents, who were in their early twenties epitomized the equitable division of child care responsibilities which characterizes the Shared Parenting model.

Example: Scott
Pattern of Shared Parenting

Scott was three years, ten months at the time of the study. His mother, age twenty-two, worked full time in an office and his father, age twenty-four, was a college student and did "odd jobs" whenever he could find part-time employment. Scott had a sister, age two-and-a-half, and both children attended the day care center connected to the father's college.

Scott was born before his mother finished high school; she remained home with him for six months, which coincided with the completion of that academic year and summer vacation. The following September she returned to school to complete her high school senior year while the father remained home to care for Scott.

Parents have continued this plan of alternating work and school, taking turns with the care of the children and with household tasks. At the time of the research study, mother worked days, while father attended school and worked intermittently weekends and vacations.

This couple was the youngest of those participating in the study, and they also were unusual in the degree to which father did cooking and other chores. He had, for example, made bread for the day care children, and made cookies for one of researcher's visits. When Scott was hungry during one of the observation visits, he announced this to his father rather than to his mother, and the father subsequently made him an eggnog. Father's involvement was reflected in the study findings in which Scott indicated almost equal preference for his mother and father in all the situations studied.

Both of Scott's parents were the eldest in large families, and both remained in contact with their parents and siblings. They seemed to feel hesitant, however, about asking for any baby-sitting help, and, in fact, only did so on a casual irregular basis. One observation occurred with Scott's paternal grandmother and three aunts, one of whom was five years old!

Role of Fathers. Several fathers in this study participated actively in the care of their children, even though their family caretaking pattern did not fall into the Shared Parenting category. While it is difficult to gauge precisely the degree of the father's involvement in routine care, we believe that at least seven of the fathers in this study took a very active role in child caring responsibilities based on the questionnaires, the researcher's observations, and the child's explicitly stated expectations. Table VII indicates our estimation of the degree and nature of involvement of the study fathers in the child's routine caretaking.

In the seven families in which the father was actively involved (Paul, Elizabeth, Steven, Scott, Kathy, James, Cindy), it appeared that his role in providing routine care was as substantial as, or exceeded, the participation of the mother.

Fathers frequently delivered the child to day care in the morning. In three families (Lori, Elizabeth and Annalee), mother and father delivered the child together; in five other families the father dropped the child off on his way to work. In two families (Paul and Steven), the father made breakfast and was responsible for getting the child ready for day care since the mother left for her work before the child got up in the morning. The mother more frequently picked the child up at day care at the end of the day. In the two families in which the parents commuted together (Lori and Elizabeth), the pick-up was done jointly. Giving dinner and putting the children to bed was the father's sole responsibility in James' family because the mother worked a late afternoon and evening shift as a saleslady.

```
┌─────────────────────────────────────────────────────────┐
│                      TABLE VII                          │
│                                                         │
│              INVOLVEMENT OF THE FATHERS                 │
│            IN THE CHILD'S ROUTINE CARETAKING            │
├─────────────────────────────────────────────────────────┤
```

| SITUATIONS | NAME OF CHILD |
|---|---|
| Delivery to Day Care | |
|     With Mother | Lori<br>*Elizabeth<br>Annalee |
|     Alone | Nina<br>*Paul<br>*Steven<br>*Scott<br>*Kathy |
| Gives Child Dinner (Mother not home) | *James |
| Reads to Child Before Bed | Elizabeth<br>Nina<br>Steven<br>Linda<br>Kathy |
| Puts Child to Bed<br>(either alone or with mother) | Steven<br>James<br>*Cindy<br>Linda<br>Ronald<br>Elizabeth<br>Kathy<br>Paul<br>Scott<br>Lori |

* Very Active Involvement

In most families bedtime preparation was an activity shared by both parents. The fathers' involvement
in the bedtime routine often consisted of reading to
the child before bedtime, and/or actually putting  the
child into bed.  Cindy's and Steven's fathers took a
very active role in the bedtime proceedings.  The ten-
derness with which Steven's father rocked the child in
his arms as he quietly sang "Rock-a-bye Steven" before
putting him in bed exuded a very special gentleness, as
illustrated in the example which follows:

Example:  Steven
Bedtime Observation:  6:45 - 8:15 P.M.

    (R=Researcher; M=Mother; F=Father;
    C=Child)

Steven was four years, three months at the
time of the study.  His mother, age thirty-
four, was a nurse and his father, age thirty-
seven, was an accountant.  Steven's brother,
Jack, was age seven.  His maternal grandmother lived in a separate apartment in the
same house.  She provided occasional, not
regular care; until recently she had been
employed out of the home and lived a very
independent life.  Mother had returned to
work when Steven was eight months old.

M and F were sitting in the living room,
reading the newspapers when R arrived.
Neither C nor his older brother was around.
R to M:  "It seems quiet here."
M to R:  "Just wait.  It's the quiet before
    the storm!  They're downstairs in
    the Rec. room."
There was a few minutes' discussion regard-
ing plans to enroll children in a day camp
with an active sports program this summer,
then M commented,
M:    "I guess it's time to start the
    ball rolling."
M went to basement door and shouted down.
M to C:  "Steven, it's time for you to
    come up now."
Immediately some very loud crying was heard,
coming from downstairs.  M began laughing
and said,
M to R:  "This happens every night."

61

C appeared in living room, still crying.
He went over and put his head in M's lap
(idiosyncratic comfort seeking behavior.)
C was dressed in his pajamas.
M to C: "What book do you want Daddy to
read tonight?"
R to C: "I brought a present for you
because this is the last time
I'm going to be coming to your
house."
C brightened as R gave him the gift (which
was a book). C got on F's lap and F began
reading to C as M discussed with R the new
bookstore in town.
When F finished the story, he said to C,
F to C: "Now it's time for bed."
M to C: "Let me clean your nose. I can't
stand a kid with a dirty nose."
C lay across M's lap while she stuck a tis-
sue up C's nose, then had him blow.
M to C: "Now give me my kiss."
C kissed M and started upstairs with F.
F to C: "Go to the bathroom."
C went to the toilet, then brushed his teeth.
F and C went into the bedroom, which C shared
with his brother, Jack. (Jack was still play-
ing downstairs—allowed to remain up later
since he is older.)
F to C: "Do I have to sing?" (Maybe em-
barrassed due to R's presence.)
C to F: "Yes."
F picked up C in his arms and began singing
and gently rocking C. The song was "Rock-a-
Bye-Baby," but instead of the word "baby" F
sang "Steven." F sang the song twice, sway-
ing slowly as he did so. C was hugging F
with his head on F's shoulder, and his legs
straddled around F's waist. F then put C
in bed and C grabbed his stuffed animal,
"Pooh."
F to C: "Goodnight. Don't get up."
F kissed C and left the room. F and R
returned to the living room where M was
lying on the floor with Jack, tearing up
wildlife stamps and pasting them in a
workbook.
F to R: "C is beginning to pick up Jack's
bad habits. In just the last
month or so he keeps getting up
after we put him to bed."

No sooner had F said this than C came to the top of stairs and said something about not liking to have the door closed.
F to C:   "You don't have to be afraid because you have Pooh."
F got up and went back upstairs and put C in again.  When F returned to the living room he said to M,
F to M:   "Your turn next."
F began reading the paper as R and M began discussing C's caretaking history.  In five to ten minutes C came to the stairs again, putting on his robe and announcing that he was freezing.
M to C:   "Well, then put on your robe and stop getting up."
M went upstairs, put C into bed again, then returned to the living room to complete the caretaker history.  No further interaction with C.

Comment:   Although Steven's parents did not fall in the category of Shared Parenting, because they had used sitters to supplement Steven's care prior to day care, it is quite clear that this father participates actively and routinely in Steven's bedtime ritual; the questionnaire indicated that he also gives both children breakfast daily and takes Steven to day care, since the mother is already at work when the children get up.

Father involvement in child care was by no means automatic, however, even in families where the mother worked full time.  Contrasted to the families in which the father assumed regular daily responsibility for various aspects of child care, there was an equal number of study families (seven) in which the father appeared to participate minimally or not at all in routine child caring duties (Matthew, Walter, Kim, John, Louis, Annalee, Nina).

Two of these seven fathers--Annalee's and Louis'— were foreign-born and perhaps had different cultural expectations regarding the paternal role.  Another two fathers—Kim's and Nina's—had work schedules which often prevented their being home at dinner and bedtime.

John and Matthew's fathers, both men in their late twenties, simply did not get involved in routine caretaking activities with their sons, both of whom were only children. These fathers, who actively conversed and sometimes teased their children and expected and received a goodnight kiss from them, left routine caretaking to the mother.

Walter's father, who was partially deaf and in his forties, seemed to view his role as that of a disciplinarian. He complained to the researcher about Walter's behavior, joined the mother in coaxing the child to eat his dinner, and several times verbally chastised the boy for not picking up his toys or not answering when spoken to. Although this father was not active in routine child care, he was clearly very much involved in the boy's socialization experience.

The value of considering the child's own perceptions of his relationships with his caretakers is illustrated by Walter's projective stories which convey a very different view of his father than was evident to the researcher during the observation visits. Walter's stories portrayed his father as a potential playmate for a game of ball, and in a tender bedtime scene, which the child made up spontaneously following the group of structured stories, enacted with family dolls. Walter's original story, recorded on tape, was spoken with convincing voice changes, to indicate the different speakers.

Example: Walter's Original Bedtime Story
Projective Doll Play Interview: Recorded

C: "And he says, 'Goodnight, Son'" (deep voice)
"Pleasant dreams" (deep voice)
"Pleasant dreams to you" (own voice)
"I love you" (deep voice)
"I love you, too" (own voice)
Smacking noises (kisses).
"The end."

Comment: Children's feelings about their parents and other caretakers may reflect both their real life experience, and their wishes or fantasies. The meaning of any relationship blends reality and idealization, and a love relationship especially involves projection of some feelings onto the partner. This perhaps is as true of the first love

relationship—that between child and parent—
as it is of mature love.

Some of the special features of the parent-child
relationship will be analyzed in Part III. The discussion which follows will explore the nature of the
child's experiences with his relatives and other sitters.

Parents Plus Relatives. Social historian, Mary Jo
Bane states that "recent sociological studies have
shown that Americans maintain close ties with many of
their relatives, and that the American nuclear family
is not as isolated from kin as was once thought....
sociologists have been showing that contemporary families have very real kinship networks."[1] This was certainly true of the families in this study, nine of whom
had frequent contact with relatives who participated
regularly in the child's care. (See Table V, #2 and
#4.) The concept of the "isolated nuclear family,"
clearly does not apply to the families who participated
in this research. Even among the eight families in
which relatives did not participate in regular child
care, six of these maintained frequent contacts in the
form of visits, phone calls or letters.

Only three of the seventeen families in this study
did not have regular contact with relatives. One of
these was the Indian child, Annalee, who responded when
asked to draw a picture of her family, "Do you mean my
family here, or my family in India?" Her resulting
drawings, when the choice was left up to her, contained
a total of eleven family members, and she is an only
child! Annalee was born in this country, of Indian
parents who have taken her with them on two occasions
when they returned to India to visit relatives.

Observation visits occurred with relatives who
provided regular caretaking for the study children,
whenever it was possible to arrange these. Eleven
grandmothers were observed with the children, five of
whom had been or still were regular caretakers, and
another five baby-sat frequently on an ad hoc basis.
Two aunts and one older sister also provided regular
caretaking and were observed in this function. The
parents were not present during these observations.

Since the grandparents played such an important role as caretakers for the families in this study, we will focus on the nature of their involvement as caretaking relatives. This discussion is based on the observation visits and also on the children's perceptions as conveyed in their doll play stories.

Role of Grandparents. Two months before her death in 1978, Margaret Mead, in an address to the American Bar Association, argued for social change that would return grandparents to the everyday lives of their grandchildren.[2] Mead had maintained in her autobiography, Blackberry Winter, that "everyone needs to have access both to grandparents and grandchildren in order to be a full human being."[3] This is similar to the position of Woodward and Kornhaber, authors of Grandparents/ Grandchildren: The Vital Connection. After interviewing three hundred children and their grandparents, these authors concluded that "the bond between grandparents and grandchildren is second in emotional power and influence only to the relationship between parents and children."[4] Observation of the children in this study who had frequent contact with their grandparents provided an optimal opportunity to understand more about this special bond.

We noted a considerable range and variety in the grandparent-grandchild relationship. Three of the grandmothers seemed to take the children for granted and did not make any special effort to interact with them (John, Scott, Matthew). These grandmothers had large families of their own, including children close in age to the grandchild, in Scott's case. There was no resemblance here to the stereotype of the doting grandparent, inclined to spoil the young child.

Two other grandmothers (Walter's and Steven's) tended to assume a rather strong, disciplinary role in their interactions with their grandchildren. Another two (Nina's and Paul's) took the role of playmate and/or educator during the observations, engaging in an elaborate tea party game on the one hand, and verbal and pencil games on the other.

Only Ronald's grandparents conveyed to us specifically and deliberately that their grandchild "was very special." This was communicated by the grandfather, who appeared to have a strong bond to the child, as demonstrated in his bragging about him and in his pleasure

66

in periodically taking Ronald to Yankee's games.
Ronald's grandfather spontaneously requested and received several kisses from the child during the observation visit.

The children's projective stories sometimes cast
the grandparent (usually grand<u>mother</u>) in a mediating
role, in which the older family member sides with the
child against a position of authority assumed by the
parent. The examples which follow, excerpted from the
projective interviews of two four-year-old children,
illustrate the flippant cliche' that the bond between
grandchild and grandparent is based on the fact that
they have a common enemy!

<u>Example A</u>:  Nina's Original Story
           (Grandmother Interaction)
<u>Projective Doll Play Interview</u>:  Recorded

C:  They're going to go back home now.
R:  OK.  You want to fix the kitchen again?
    What's going to happen in the kitchen?
C:  They're going to cook.
R:  Who's going to cook?
C:  The Mommy.  The Gramma's going to help
    her.
R:  And what's Daddy going to do?
C:  Daddy's going to sit down at the table.
    And then Daddy gets mad because the
    little girl hit him.
R:  Why did she hit Daddy?
C:  Because she didn't want to come back.
R:  She wasn't ready to come back yet.
C:  She wants to still watch the monkeys.
    (Relates to zoo story which preceeded
    this.)
R:  She hit Daddy, and what did Daddy do?
C:  Spank her.
R:  Daddy spanked her.  And what did he say
    to her?
C:  Go up to your room.
R:  And what is she going to do?

C:  Go up to her room.
R:  Is she crying?
C:  Yep.  (Ohhh—whiny noise)
R:  "I wanted to watch the monkeys."  And
    then what?  What does Mommy say?
C:  Go up to your room.

67

R: And then what happens?
C: The little boy cries.
R: Why is the little boy crying?
C: Because he wants the little girl.
R: Oh, he misses his friend. And what did the Daddy say to the little boy?
C: You can't see your friend.
R: Why?
C: Cause she was bad.
R: Why was she bad? —she's my friend.
C: Cause she hit Daddy because she wanted to see the monkeys.
R: And then what's Gramma going to do?
C: She's not gonna do nothing.
R: No? She's not going to do anything, or say anything?
C: No.
R: And then what happens next?
C: The little girl comes down by herself when no one tells her.
R: Oh. And what's she going to do?
C: The Mother's going to send her up to her room again.
R: Again? Oh.
C: The Gramma's going to take her up to her room. The Gramma's going to kiss her. (Smacking noises.)
R: And does Gramma come back downstairs? Hum?
C: Yep.
R: And what does Gramma say?
C: Good-night.
R: So then what's Mommy going to do?
C: She's not going to do anything.
R: OK. Is Daddy going to do anything?
C: No.

Comment: Note the role of the grandmother in this story as providing comfort to the child, when both Mother and Father were united in their disciplinary stance.


The next story portrays the grandmother as actively intervening between child and parents.

68

Example B: Walter (Grandmother Interaction)
Projective Doll Play Interview: Nurturance Theme

R: What happens next? You finish the story.
C: And he drops the milk. And he spills it.
R: And then what does the Mommy say?
C: (Funny voice) Go in your room.
R: And what does the Daddy say?
C: (Strong voice) And stay there.
R: And what does the Gramma say?
C: (High pitched voice) Don't make the
little boy...(interruption)
R: And isn't he going to have any supper?
C: (Shook head No.)
R: No? He's going to be so hungry. He
isn't going to have any supper?
C: No. (Long pause.) So he said, "I'm
sorry, Mom." So he come out and play
on the rocking chair. The end.
R: It couldn't be the end because it's time
for dinner. Who does the boy sit next
to at the table? (Proximity)
C: Daddy.
R: And who's on the other side?
C: Gramma.
R: And do they have a nice supper together?
C: Yeah.

Two of the study children, including Walter, knew
their grandparents phone numbers by heart, and occasionally spontaneously phoned them at various times of
the day and night (6:00 a.m. was a favorite time for
Walter). Another child's independent play in the
Introductory visit revealed interest in both of her
grandmothers and her desire to be close to them.
Kathy built a large structure with dominoes and when
asked what it was, stated: "It's a big apartment
building where me and my two grandmothers live."

This desire of preschoolers for proximity with the
older generation may not be shared by their parents,
some of whom may prefer to avoid proximity (and thereby
avoid possible advice and criticism from their elders.)
This was a finding of The Working Family Project at
Harvard University which studied fourteen dual-worker
families with respect to their feelings about parenthood.[5] Since our research focused on the children,
we do not know how the parents in our study felt about
their frequent dependence on the grandparents for child

care. Among the children, however, the consensus was
unanimous. Grandparents were never viewed by them as
unfriendly, hostile or nonsupportive; rather, they
typically assumed mediating, influential and supportive
positions on the child's behalf.

Other Caretaking Relatives. We observed two teen-age
aunts, and one teen-age sibling in their regular caretaking roles with the children. The behavior of these
girls was similar to that of the unrelated sitters,
which will be discussed next.

Parents Plus Unrelated Sitters. When family members
do not live close or are unavailable to help with
child care, the family often resorts to purchasing
care from friends, neighbors or unrelated sitters.
Three of the five families in this study who purchased
child care obtained the services of friends of the
mothers to care for their children. These were "older"
women who had children of their own, either close in
age to the study child (which meant that the children
were playmates for each other), or in other instances,
the sitter's children were school age and would usually
help with the caretaking when they returned from school.

> Example: Elizabeth (Sitter Interaction #1)
> Observation Visit: Sitter's Home—5:30 -
>                      6:30 p.m.

Elizabeth was four years, two months at
the time of the study. Her mother, age
thirty-eight, had an administrative position in a bank and her father, age forty-
four, was a business executive. Elizabeth
had a brother, eighteen months old. Mother
had returned to work three days per week
when Elizabeth was two months old, leaving the baby with an unrelated sitter at
home. From the time Elizabeth was about
two years old, parents left her daily with
a neighbor who takes her to day care and
picks her up there. The parents work day
is long; they leave before day care opens,
and return after it closes. The neighbor
has a twelve-year-old daughter who shares
in the caretaking. On the questionnaire,
Elizabeth's mother referred to the long-
term sitter as Elizabeth's "second mother,"
and the sitter referred to Elizabeth as
"one of the family."

(C=Child; R-Researcher; S=Sitter; B=Baby- [sib] )

This observation began in the bathroom, where
S's eighth grade daughter was giving a bath
to C and B.

S to R:   "It's easier for their parents if
          we give the kids their baths here.
          Then they go home in their night
          clothes, have dinner and are all
          ready for bed."

C to R:   "We have bubble bath."

There was some discussion about a suction
soap holder on the side of the tub. After
about five minutes S took B out of the tub
and carried him into the bedroom. C remained in the tub by herself and R remained
in the bathroom with her.

C to R:   "I'm keeping you company."

After maybe five minutes more, C decided to
get out. She carefully wrang the water out
of the wash cloth, then got out, wrapped herself in a towel, and ran into the bedroom.
B was now dressed in a blanket sleeper. C
sat on the bed and waited for S to help her
dress. C was shivering as S put on C's
undershirt, underpants, nightgown and robe.
Then S brushed C's hair. C asked if she
could wear a barrette. S said, "Yes." C
got up, opened the dressing table drawer
and chose an orange barrette. S put it in
C's hair. C then began playing with the
make-up mirror on the dressing table. C
showed R its two sides, one of which was a
magnifying mirror and which C seemed to enjoy. S said, "Let's go downstairs now."
There was the sound of a cello coming from
downstairs.

We went downstairs (C, R and S). As we
went into the living room we saw S's husband playing the cello with B on his knee.
C walked over and watched as they played.
S was filling out the questionnaire at the
dining room table. C plucked the strings of
the cello, B got down and S's husband put
the cello away in the corner. S's husband
said to C:

> "We discovered a bird's nest with
> some baby birds in it. If you are
> very quiet and don't frighten the
> mother bird, you can see it."

Husband took C to the front door and held her
up to see the nest which had been made in a
straw cornucopia, in the midst of an arrangement of plastic flowers.
M arrived.
C said to her:

> "We made popcorn balls today at
> school." (This was the same state-
> ment with which C had greeted R and
> S.)

M to C: "That's sounds great."
As B toddled over to the cello in the corner
there was some talk about how he had helped
husband practice. M picked up B but he
arched his back and whined and M put him
down. F came in.
B to F: "Hi."
C to F: "There's a nest of baby birds by
the door."
F went to look with C following him closely.
F held C by her hands and C did a gymnastic
trick, turning a somersault.
F said: "C is very good in gymnastics."

There was some transfer of clothing in a
plastic picnic bag being used to carry dia-
pers. C asked S if she could wear the barrette home. S said, "Yes." Family left
and R followed them home for dinner observation.

Few families have such a long-term, seemingly ideal
child care arrangement for their children. Many end
up trying several different sitters, with teen-agers
frequently serving in this capacity for families that
need sitters evenings or on Saturdays.

We observed a total of five teen-age sitters who
regularly cared for the study children. Their interactions were quite different from those of the grandmothers or "older women" who tended to be rather low
key, by comparison. The girls engaged the children in
a variety of activities, such as cards, board games,
drawing or fantasy play. The one male teen-age sitter

we observed played quite actively with the male child (John), arm wrestling, tusseling and teasing him to the point the child protested and threatened to tell his parents.

An interaction with a beloved teen-age sitter is illustrated below:

Example: Elizabeth (Sitter Interaction #2)
Observation Visit: Family Home—7:30 - 8:30 p.m.

Arrived on time; the inside door had been left open as if family were expecting some-one. F came downstairs to let R in. No-body seemed to be around. F said that the sitter was here. F and R talked for a few minutes, standing in the hallway, then S came down the stairs carrying brother, who was dressed in a pink blanket sleeper and smiling as usual. Brother said "Hi" to R, one of his most frequently used words. F introduced R to S. C came running down the steps. She was dressed in a long bath-robe and slippers. C said "Hi" to R, but seemed most intent on getting involved in playing with S. S is a nice-looking teen-ager of fifteen or sixteen years who was dressed in typical adolescent garb.

S put B in playpen.
C said,  "I have marbles" (holding up a
         green felt bag)—do you want to
         play?"
R to C:  "OK," thinking C was addressing
         her, but C replied,
         "I wasn't talking to you, I was
         talking to S."
S to C:  "OK. I'll play."
C and S knelt down on the rug. R sat on the couch and watched. C dumped the marbles out.
C said:  "Let's play 'going to the bathroom'
         like we did before."
C looked at R and giggled. C held up the marbles in her fist and let them drop one by one on the rug.
C said:  "Plop, plop, plop," and giggled
         again. S giggled with C.

73

C to R:  "Doesn't that sound like going to
          the bathroom?"
R to C:  (Smiling) "I guess it does."
C to S:  "Let's put them inside, the way we
          did before," (giggling).
C and S put the marbles into the neck of C's
robe.  C then stood up, and the marbles dropped
down.  C gave out peals of laughter, and wanted
to repeat this game over and over.  They played
it for about ten minutes, and then C said,

> "Let's play something else; let's
> pretend you're the Mommy and I'm
> the baby, and after I go to sleep,
> you go away, and then I wake up and
> can't find you." (*ON: fear of
> abandonment.)

C and S each sat in a separate chair, closed
their eyes and then S got up and crept away,
going into the living room (where F had been
sitting all of this time reading the paper).
C "woke up," looked around, got up and started
calling,

> "Mommy, Mommy, where are you?"

C ran around from room to room calling, "Mommy,
where are you?" and then shouting and laughing
with glee when she discovered S hiding.  C and
S then reversed roles and repeated the game,
this time with S as the mother and C as the
baby.  (*ON: A form of "Hide and Seek"—
Baby/Mother version.)  When C (baby) ran away
and hid, S called out, "Baby, baby where are
you?"  Again, there was a lot of squealing
and laughing when the hiding person was discovered.

M came in during this play.  She took brother
out of the playpen and took him into the kitchen to give him some medicine.  F said to M
that he was ready to go.  M told S where the
telephone number was, where they could be
reached.  M also told S that they would not
be late, and that C should go to bed at
8:30.  S asked if C could eat something before
bed.
M said:  "The kitchen is closed; she can have
          some juice if she wants something."

---

*ON:  Observation Note

M put the baby to bed and parents both left,
very matter-of-factly—neither one said anything directly to C, nor did either one kiss
her good-bye.

After parents left, C said to S:
     "Let's make up some stories."
C to S:  "You talk to me in Spanish and I'll
     talk to you in English."
S began to encourage C to repeat words and
phrases after her in Spanish.  C was not too
interested in this.  C said:
     "I'm going to talk my language and
     you repeat it after me."
C began speaking in jibberish-jargon sentences,
pausing for S to repeat.  C and S giggled a
lot as they did this for about ten minutes.

<u>Parents Plus Relatives Plus Unrelated Sitters</u>.  This
model of child care gives the child the widest range
of caretaking experiences and was the pattern used
by the majority (seven) of the study families.  Offer-
ing maximum flexibility and variety for both child and
family, the pattern can be pictured as a network of
protective spheres encircling the child, who is the
nucleus of the matrix.  (See Figure 1.)

Since we assume that children are capable of
forming a wide range of attachments, and that, to a
certain extent, opportunity determines attachment
formation, this model offers the diversity of a broad
social network, plus the security of kinship ties.

It would represent the ideal to Margaret Mead who
believed that "the family, widely assisted by grandparents, aunts and uncles, neighbors and friends, and
supplemented by more varied experiences in other settings, provides the context in which children are best
reared to become full human beings."[6]

<u>Mixed with Minimal Involvement of Father</u>.  Some fathers
do not involve themselves with routine child care responsibilities.  In these families the mother assumes
the brunt of child care duties, and arranges substitute
care in her absence. As discussed previously (pp. 63-64)
paternal non-involvement may be motivated by cultural,
logistical, or age factors.  However, no definitive
conclusions can be drawn without further study.

Figure 1  EXPANDING  CARETAKING  SPHERES

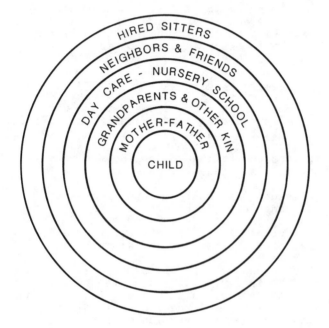

# NOTES

1. Bane, Mary Jo, _Here to Stay: American Families in the Twentieth Century_ (New York: Basic Books) 1976, p. 37.

2. Mead, Margaret, Address to American Bar Association, Chicago, September 5, 1978.

3. Mead, Margaret, _Blackberry Winter_ (New York: Morrow) 1972, p. 328.

4. Woodward, Kenneth and Kornhaber, Arthur, "Where Have All the Grandparents Gone?" _The New York Times_, May 10, 1981. _____, _Grandparents/ Grandchildren: The Vital Connection_ (Garden City, New York: Doubleday) 1981.

5. Working Family Project, in _Working Couples_, Robert and Rhona Rapaport, eds. (New York: Harper & Row) 1978, p. 79.

6. Mead, Margaret, _Blackberry Winter_, op. cit., p. 324.

# III  SCRUTINIZING THE PARENT-CHILD RELATIONSHIP
FOR CLUES ABOUT ATTACHMENT

# III SCRUTINIZING THE PARENT-CHILD RELATIONSHIP FOR CLUES ABOUT ATTACHMENT

Attachment relationships are enduring, positive bonds binding individuals to each other with a connection that is reciprocal and compelling. How does this attachment bond get translated into behavior? How do we know an attachment exists between two people? The question is deceptively simple if we consider that the subject of love (here a synonym of attachment) has intrigued poets and mystified philosophers for centuries. The very elusiveness of the idea of love and its ineffable qualities seems to evade precise description and examination.

If a researcher studied an adult man or woman, looking for differences in their relationships with their spouse, children, brothers, sisters, parents and colleagues, would <u>observable</u>, <u>distinctive</u> <u>behaviors</u> be evident in the different interactions? Although the adult might really "love" all of these individuals, would not the precise <u>nature</u> and expression of the love be quite different in regard to each? Of course the adult could tell the researcher about his or her underlying feelings, and the researcher could then compare the adult's statements with the behavior with different individuals. Since self-reflection and comparative evaluation is beyond the scope of a four or five-year-old child, we are, therefore, more dependent on behavioral cues in looking for indications of the young child's underlying attachment bonds.

In thinking about how four and five-year-olds would be apt to express their attachment (love) feelings toward their various caretakers, we did not expect separation protest to be significant, since older preschoolers have an internalized image of their parents (object constancy) and know, based on their life experience with repeated separations, that people who leave usually come back.

We thought, however, that the other "major indicator of attachment"—proximity-seeking—might continue to be a valid signal of attachment for the preschool child since positive feelings, even in adults, typically arouse the desire to be with the loved individual as much as possible.

We translated proximity-seeking into "preference for the company of a specific person," and then incorporated element of choice and selectivity in our three methods of studying attachment. The Questionnaires sought the opinions of the important people in the child's life regarding whom the child would prefer to have care for him or her in different situations. The child, in the Projective Stories, had the opportunity to set up various caretaking situations according to his own wishes for contact with different caretakers in stress and play situations. Third, the research Observations occurred during real-life situations in which the child's proximity to and preferences for different caretakers were visible in on-the-spot transactions.

Mary Ainsworth, in a letter to the author in 1977, referred to Harlow's categorization of five types of "affectional relationships" for rhesus monkeys,[1] stating her belief that human relationships also differ significantly both in kind and degree among the infant's principal caregivers. Our study enabled us to study close-ups of the child's interactions with different people in different situations so that similarities, contrasts and distinctions among various relationships zoomed into focus.

After determining the attachment preferences of our study group of children of working parents we planned to study intensively the nature of the interactions between the child and his or her primary attachment ties. We wanted to uncover and understand the underlying reasons for the existence and persistence of these special bonds.

This speculative discussion, illustrated with examples from the small research sample, draws on the author's many years of professional experience working with hundreds of parents and young children. We believe that our theoretical ideas have implications for understanding the very core of the attachment process itself: on what is it based and why is it so persistent.

Attachment to Parents. A major finding of this research is that the study children showed strong preferences for their mothers and fathers in all situations, based on the children's caretaking preferences as rated in the Questionnaires, Observations and Projective Interviews.

The data analysis consisted of tallying the question-naires, the children's selection and spontaneous refer-ences to specific caretakers in the projective stories, and coding child-caretaker interactions and prevailing themes in the observational field notes. Details of this data analysis, available elsewhere,[2] will not be repeated here.

Our attention now pivots toward and rivets on the parent-child interaction, scrutinizing it closely to discover clues as to its singular qualities which en-dure despite little shared time for working parent and child to nourish their relationship. We wanted to find the key to the survival of this bond, which we believed must, in fact, be different in essence, from the child's attachments to other caretakers.

Examination and diligent study of our observational field notes revealed three unique aspects of the parent-child interaction which differentiate it from the child's relationships with other caretakers. These special characteristics will be discussed separately in the chapters which follow:

NOTES

1. See, Harlow, Harry, Learning to Love (New York: Ballantine Books) 1971.

   Ainsworth, citing Harlow, specified five different kinds of "affectional relationships" for rhesus monkeys:

      (1) infant to mother
      (2) mother to infant
      (3) infant to infant (or peer to age peer)
      (4) heterosexual relations
      (5) adult male to infant

2. Webb, Nancy Boyd, Attachment Relationships of Pre-
   schoolers to Parents and Other Familiar Caretakers:
   Implications for Day Care and Working Mothers
   (Unpublished doctoral dissertation, Columbia
   University School of Social Work, New York)
   1979, Ann Arbor, MI: University Microfilms.

## Chapter Five

## NUDGING AND BUGGING

Attachment is a two-way process, with the behavior of one person touching and affecting that of the other, and vice versa. We have considered the impact of the child's "intrinsic interactive style" on all caretaking interactions, and we have discussed some specific features of the grandparents' and sitters' involvement with the child. Our focus will now shift to the input of the parents.

One hundred and twenty-five hours spent observing nineteen children with eighty different caretakers (parents, relatives, teachers and sitters) convinced us that some relationships had a low key and passive quality, while others seemed more vital and charged with emotion. This was very evident, for example, in observations of the child's change in behavior when the parents picked him or her up at the day care center or at the sitter's. Despite the child's basic interactive style, which prevails across relationships, there was often a distinct difference in the feeling tone among the different relationships. Our day care observation visit which occurred at the end of the day usually included the parent's pick-up of the child, followed by returning home for the family dinner. This sequence of observations enabled us to track the child <u>on the same day</u> with several different caretakers. We believe that some of the differences evident in the interactions were related to the nature of the <u>adult's</u> input, based on the adult's attachment to the child.

We noticed a striking difference in the <u>amount</u> of interaction with the children initiated by various caretakers. During some observations, for example, the caretaker almost ignored the child, and interactions were basically left to the child to initiate (this was true in observations of several of the children with their grandmothers: John, Matthew, and Scott). By contrast, many of the observations of the children with the parents seemed to take the form of the parents almost constantly initiating involvement with the child.

We wondered if the parents' reactions might be related to the effects of being observed and to the

parents' desire to have their children appear in a
favorable light ("Observer Effects").  This would explain the parents' prompting the child with comments
such as"  "Show Mrs. Webb what you made in school today," or "Tell Mrs. Webb how you took your bath all by
yourself yesterday."

However, other types of interactions came across
as sternly disciplinary or critical, almost embarrass-
ingly intimate, and seemed oblivious and unrelated to
the presence of an observer.  Angry comments such as,
"Stop playing with your food or I'm going to send you
to your room!" (Walter's mother at dinner), and "Cry
louder, I can't hear you!" (said sarcastically to Lori
by her father when she began having a tantrum after
being denied a cookie before dinner), seemed to indicate that many behaviors and interactions were not cen-
sored by the parents nor enhanced for the observer's
benefit.

Caretaker Impingement: Nudging and Bugging.  We called
the caretaker input into the interaction "caretaker impingement," defining the term according to Webster's
definition of impingement as behavior which influences,
effects, encroaches and infringes.  We privately thought
of this concept as "bugging" and "nudging"—expressions
which convey the nagging quality sometimes quite evident in the term "caretaker impingement."  However,
the impinging can have a positive quality, including
proud and affectionate behaviors and statements.

The color coded field notes highlighted every instance in which a caretaker initiated an interaction
with a child (and vice versa), specifying whether this
was verbal or behavioral, and the nature of any accompanying positive or negative emotion.  (See Appendix
for complete Coding Guide.)  This color coding enabled
us to study the quality of the interaction, including
the manner in which the caretaker responded to the
child.  It also facilitated comparisons between different caretakers.

Our impression based on the observations had been
that mothers and fathers did more nudging and bugging
than other caretakers, and the coding bore this out.
While all caretaking adults impinge to some degree on
children in the process of disciplining them and en-
couraging desirable behavior, parents in our study
(especially mothers) did this much more often than did

86

other caretakers.  The following examples give a flavor
of these impinging interactions, which as previously
indicated can be either positive or negative.


Direct VERBAL Impingement*
Name of Child:  Steven

(Father arrived home and came into the
living room where the children were lying on the floor, coloring and intermittently watching "Godzilla" on TV.)

F:  "I didn't know  Steven was going to be
on TV tonight!"


Direct VERBAL and BEHAVIORAL Impingement
Name of Child:  Elizabeth

(F put out his hands and Elizabeth performed a somersault trick by holding on
and turning upside down.)

F:  "Elizabeth is very good at gynmastics."


---

* Direct Caretaker Impingement consists
of verbal and behavioral comments and
activities on the part of the caretaker which are directed to the child in
such a way as to stimulate an interaction.  These include:  (verbal) spontaneous positive, negative or neutral
comments, including praise, information-
giving, sarcasm and teasing, and
(behavioral) instances of the caretaker initiating play, routine tasks, or
affectionate behaviors with the child.

Direct BEHAVIORAL Impingement
Name of Child: James

(At day care center. Mother came to pick child
up at end of day. Children were playing outdoors; the driveway is adjacent to play area.)

C, who was standing near R, watched his
mother drive up.
C said to himself or to R: "Why so early?"
Then he ran inside to get his jacket and
school papers.
M came over to R and said, "Hello."
C then ran up to M. M ruffled C's hair and
said to C: "Hi Ya, Jim."
M said "Good-bye" to R.
C and M walked together toward the car. M
had her arm across C's shoulders, and she
seemed to be rubbing his back as they walked,
with her head bent listening to something he
was telling her.

Direct BEHAVIORAL Impingement
Name of Child: Steven

(At day care center. End of day. Mother
came to pick up child. Children playing
outside. M, who had come directly from
work, was wearing her nurse's uniform."

C saw M arrive and immediately ran and jumped
on the "Merry-go-round" (playground equipment).
M looked at R and said, "You see how he re-
acts to me!"
M went into the Center where the older children (C's sibling) were involved in an indoor activity. M and sib quickly came out
and sib ran and immediately got into the car.
M went over to the Merry-go-round where C
was standing with his back to the play area.
M jumped on the Merry-go-round, grabbed C
under her arm, and carried him in her arms
back to the car.

Caretakers "impinge" on children either <u>directly</u>
(as in examples above by giving the child a kiss or a
slap or saying something to start an interaction), or
<u>indirectly</u> (trying to motivate the child to change or
modify his or her own behavior). Indirect impingement
represents a potential source of stress since the

outcome depends on the child's willingness to comply with the caretaker's request. The truism that it is easier to do something oneself than to get someone else to do it is relevant here.

Verbal and behavioral impingement often occur together and sometimes there is overlap also between the concepts of direct and indirect impingement. However, even though the categories may not be exclusive, there is a clear distinction between the caretaker's direct action on the child and the caretaker's attempting to instigate the child to act, as in the examples of indirect caretaker impingement, which follow:

> Indirect VERBAL and BEHAVIORAL Impingement*
> Coaxing and Scolding and Hitting
> Name of Child:   Matthew
>
> (During bedtime observation.)
>
> M to C:   "Can you untie your shoes?"
> C to M:   "No."
> M hit C sharply on the leg.
> M to C:   Matthew, you know you can!"
> C untied the shoe, but got a knot in it.
> M (irritated) to C:   "You can do better than
>                that!  You don't have to get knots
>                in your shoes!"
> C to M:   "You do the other one."
> M to C:   "No!  You do it."
> C did it.

---

*Indirect Caretaker Impingement consists of verbal and behavioral comments and activities which have the purpose of motivating the child to control or modify his or her own behavior according to the manner suggested by the caretaker. This may take the form of asking the child to do something such as a routine task, or of suggesting that the child show, tell, perform or display a skill or work. Coaxing the child to eat, behave, wash or toilet is also included in this category as are socializing and disciplining behaviors such as threatening, denying ("Don't do that"), scolding and hitting. Asking the child for kisses or hugs would also be considered a form of indirect caretaker impingement.

Indirect VERBAL Impingement
Asking Child to Do Something
Name of Child: Louis

(Dinner Observation; before dinner; family is
together in family room. Father, arriving
from work, is heard pulling his car into the
garage.)

M to C: "Daddy's home. Do you want to hide?"
C to M: "No." (involved in play with a fire
      truck)
M to C: "You always do. Hurry up, before
      he comes in!"
C hid behind chair. F came in and said "Hello"
to R.
M whispered to F re. C hiding.
F: "Where's Louis?"
M to F: "I don't know, he was here a few
      minutes ago."
C jumped out from behind the chair and said,
      "Here I am!"
F went over to C and patted his head.


Indirect VERBAL Impingement
Asking Child to Show and Scolding
Name of Child: Kathy

(During Bedtime Observation; family is together
in living room. Mother is holding infant, getting ready to nurse it; C sat down on the coffee table.)

M to C: "Don't put your feet on the table,
      Kathy, we're trying to sell it!"
C continued to scoot around the table and
then climbed on the couch, pushing herself
up by bracing her feet on the coffee table.
M to C (more firmly, and with some anger):
      "Kathy, I _said_ don't put your feet
      on the table! Come over and sit
      by me. Did you show Mrs. Webb
      your necklace and tell her where
      you got it?"
C to R: "It's from Grace" (touching the
      necklace and smiling slightly).
M to C: "Mrs. Webb doesn't know who Grace
      is—you'll have to tell her."

C said nothing.
M to C: "Mrs. Webb doesn't know if Grace is
        your friend or mine."
C to M: "She's your friend—at your school."
A few minutes later, M to C:
        "Do you have sand in your shoes?"
C's shoes looked dusty, as if she had been
playing in dirt.
C to M: "I shook it out."
M to C: "Where did you shake the sand?"
C pointed to a corner of the living room.
M to C: (in disgust)
        "Kathy!! Where does Mommy put the
        sand when she shakes out your shoes?"
C to M: "Outside.
M to C: "Or in the basket....<u>don't you ever
        shake it on the rug again!</u>"
C lowered her head and looked as if she was
about to cry.


<u>Indirect VERBAL and BEHAVIORAL Impingement</u>
Asking for Affectionate Display
Name of Child: Ronald

(GF=Grandfather; GM=Grandmother)

(During Sitter Observation with maternal
grandparents. It was Father's Day and the
family had just completed a backyard picnic. An aunt and a friend of the aunt's
were also present. A TV set had been placed
on one end of the picnic table, and when R
arrived C was sitting on GF's lap, watching
TV with him.)

R went over to C and GF, introduced herself
to GF and remarked that they seemed to be
enjoying watching the baseball game together.
GF to R: "Ron and I are going to go to a
         Yankees game together."
C said nothing, but got down and began playing with a big truck nearby.
GF said he was willing to answer any questions about C, but he didn't have his reading glasses, so R would have to fill in the
questionnaire for him. As GF responded verbally to the questionnaire, it became evident
that C was very special to him. At one point,

91

GF said to C:
          "Come here and give me a kiss."
C scrambled up on GF's lap and kissed and
hugged him.
GM to R: "He's not that affectionate with
          me! I think it's because I'm
          always working around the house,
          whereas GF is free to play with
          him."


The term "unsolicited impingement" obviously includes a wide range of behaviors and verbalizations.
We wondered why it might be that parents in our study
nudged and bugged so much more than did other caretakers. Our considered opinion is that this behavior
is a reflection of underlying feelings of closeness,
concern, interest and love (i.e., attachment). We
propose that the impinging means that the child is
very important to the adult, who otherwise would not
bother so extensively with the often tedious process
of socialization. The "failure to thrive" child, in
fact, often has had the opposite experience—no one
cared enough to nudge or impinge in any consistent or
meaningful way. This idea is similar to Urie Bronfenbrenner's notion that a child needs the "enduring,
irrational involvement of one or more adults" and the
conviction that someone cares for him or her in a
totally unquestionable manner!

          In essence, we are suggesting that the attachment
bond originating in the adult, gets transformed into
impinging behavior which communicates to the child a
sense of his or her significance, and, ultimately leads
to reciprocity in the child-to-adult attachment relationship. The mother who coaxes the child to finish
his or her dinner, or urges the child to eat more,
says implicitly to the child, "You are important to
me, therefore I want you to eat and be strong and
healthy." We will consider the bonding effects of
proprietary feelings in greater detail in Chapter Seven.

Maternal and Paternal Interactions. Comparisons of
maternal and paternal interactions with infants and
young children have demonstrated consistent differences
in the manner in which mothers and fathers relate to
their children. Berry Brazelton, who studied early parent-infant reciprocity, found that "an infant by two or
three weeks displays an entirely different attitude

(more wide-eyed, playful and bright-faced) toward his father than to his mother."[2]  Similarly, Michael Lamb found distinctions in parental behavior, particularly in regard to the type of play initiated by each. Lamb states:

> The fathers were more likely to engage in idiosyncratic and rough-and-tumble types of play, and it may be because of the greater variety and unpredictability of the play with the fathers that the response to play with them was more positive than with the mothers... The mothers held the infants far more than the fathers did, but this was usually for caretaking or controlling the infant's activities. They seldom picked up or held the infants for play, whereas infants were held by their fathers most often for this purpose.[3]

Our study showed similar distinctions in the nature of maternal and paternal interactions. All of the caretakers were asked, on the Questionnaire, to list any special activities which the child liked to engage in with them. The responses to this question Table VIII, "Special Activities Engaged in by Study Children and Various Caretakers") indicate an equivalent number of activities listed by mothers and fathers. A close look at the type activity, however, shows that the fathers mentioned physical activities and sports with much greater frequency than did the mothers. This is consistent with our impressions during the observations that the fathers tended to engage in physical exercise—or sports—activities with both their male and female children. Elizabeth's interest in gymnastics, for example, was clearly encouraged by her father, who greeted her at the end of the day by holding out his hands to support her somersault trick, after which he commented that she was very good in gymnastics. Kathy's father also encouraged his daughter's gymnastic interests, and Cindy's father earnestly helped her improve her baseball batting skills.

We could not recall nor locate in our field notes a single instance of a maternal-child interaction which

## TABLE VIII

### "SPECIAL ACTIVITIES" ENGAGED IN
### BY STUDY CHILDREN AND VARIOUS CARETAKERS*

| Father | Mother |
|---|---|
| Help cook | Singing in car |
| Bike riding | Reading and cooking |
| Sports or physical activities | Reading |
| | Singing |
| Fixing anything mechanical and playing soccer | Preparing meals and grocery shopping |
| Fishing and baseball | Games of concentration or Fish (cards) |
| Games - music | Taking a walk |
| Story | Taking a nap |
| Word games | Shopping |
| Hide and seek | |
| Going out to dinner | |

| Grandfather | Grandmother |
|---|---|
| "Go to Yankee's game and eat hot dogs." | "He sits on a stool and supervises me making lunch." |

### Sitters

Games-soccer (older sibling)
Looking around my room (aunt)
Talking
Reading a book
Reading, pretending and silly games

*Based on items written in by fifty-six Questionnaire respondents.

could be categorized as a large muscle or sports activity, even in the case of the one mother who was a physical education teacher! One bedtime observation included all members of a family dancing together, but even though the mother had put on the record initiating the activity, it was the father who held the child's hands and "danced" with his daughter (Lori).

In addition to physical interactions, the fathers in this study tended to tease their children and use sarcasm more often than did the mothers. We have given examples of this with regard to Steven's and Lori's fathers.

The involvement of the mothers with their children took the form of cooking, singing, reading, games of concentration and shopping. The same pattern of sex-based differences in types of interactions also characterized the sitters in our study, with male sitters favoring physical play, and female sitters preferring quiet games.

Our findings indicated the children's equal preferences for mother and father at <u>Bedtime</u>, and a slight preference for the father in <u>Play</u> situations. This reflects the reality of their experience, to some extent. In all other situations (Hurt, Nurturance and Fear), the mother was preferred. In the <u>Hurt</u> situations she was preferred three times as often as the father, and in the <u>Fear</u> situation she was chosen twice as often.

We were interested in how the caretaker's behavior might influence the child's preferences. In Schaffer and Emerson's[4] study of development of social attachments in infancy, they identified two variables which were significantly related to the intensity of attachment to the mother among their sample of infants up to eighteen months of age. These were:

1. the nature of responsiveness to the child (degree and speed of maternal reaction in relation to the child's crying), and
2. the amount of interaction with the child.

Our color coding and tabulation included a category of <u>Caretaker Responsiveness</u> in which we itemized who initiated the interaction (caretaker or child), and the nature of the response which followed (whether it was reciprocal* or complementary*) in addition to the accompanying emotions, and whether the response was verbal or behavioral, and whether positive, negative or neutral.

There was definitely more activity and involvement with the study children on the part of the mothers and fathers in this research than originated from the other caretakers. Complementary interactions were much more common in the parent-child relationship (and in the teacher-child relationship) than in the child's interactions with other caretakers.

It would be questionable, however, to conclude that complementary or impinging relationships promote attachment, based on the fact that the study children indicated more preferences for their mothers, and their mothers engage in more impinging and complementary type interactions with their children. Causality cannot be inferred based on co-existing, and possibly coincidental, factors.

The intent of this study was not to determine causality, which would be an inappropriate goal in exploratory research. We sought, rather to explore the element of reciprocity (mutuality) as a factor which might contribute to the significance and persistence of a relationship.

This is a very complex matter. We identified instances when too much impinging stimulation from a parent resulted in oppositional behavior (Kathy, Lori). We also noted that most of the study grandmothers were relatively uninvolved in interactions with their grandchildren, although they spent a lot of time with them.

---

*Reciprocity refers to the quality of mutuality in an interaction "in which the participants show similar behavior, either simultaneously or alternatively."[5]
*Complementary interactions describe transactions in which "the behavior of one differs from, but complements, that of the other,"[6] (as in feeding and eating).

The children preferred their grandmothers as sitters,
however, despite their minimal involvement. Sitters
and fathers each played with the children in a reciprocal fashion which the children very much enjoyed.
However, only two children (Elizabeth and Louis) selected sitters as preferred caretakers as frequently as
they did their fathers. These two instances included
Louis' sixteen-year-old sister, and Elizabeth's daily
contact with her sitter over a three-year interval,
relationships not typical of the usual sitter-child
interaction. We believe that children's awareness of
family bonds may be significant in their attachment
preferences. This will be discussed further in Chapter
Seven.

While Schaffer and Emerson's variable "caretaker
responsiveness" seems to show some relationship to the
children's preferences for mother and father, it is not
clear how this relates to sitters, grandmothers and
other relatives. We conclude that factors other than
caretaker responsiveness contribute to the development
of attachment, and we speculate that the behavior of
the caretaker toward the child plays a crucial role in
communicating to the child the importance of their
special relationship.

We know that infants are not born "attached" to
any one caretaker. The state of becoming attached
evolves over time as the baby learns to distinguish
self from non-self, and to discriminate among specific
individuals. Ainsworth indicates that "attachments are
learned"[7] and Bowlby stresses that while the potential
for the development of attachment is innate, the actual
nature and form of the relationships depends on the
environment.[8]

A gradual evolution from diffuse to more discriminating attachment responses characterizes the sequen-
tial phases in the typical development of attachment
relationships.

Schaffer identified two broad phases of social
development, namely, "indiscriminate attachment orien-
tation towards social objects," followed by specific
attachments (around seven months of age), satisfied
only by the presence of one or two individuals.
Schaffer suggests the origins of attachment behavior
as the infant's gradual learning of "the special stimulating properties inherent in his human partners,

(causing him) to distinguish them as a class in their own right, (and to) seek their physical proximity in order to be exposed to their relatively high and accommodating arousal value. The infant protests when he is prevented from achieving this end."9

A more detailed schema, presented by Yarrow, outlined four steps in the development of "focused relationships," a term synonymous with attachment. The steps in this progression are:

1. Social Awareness (Discrimination of People and Objects)
2. Active Recognition of Mother
3. Preference for the Mother over Strangers
4. The Development of Specific Expectations towards the Mother: The Confidence Relationship.11

On the basis of home observations and parent interviews, Yarrow charted the developmental course of attachment in one hundred infants from one to eight months of age. Stage 1 was achieved by sixty-five percent of the infants by one month of age, Stage 2 by eighty-one percent of the infants by three months, Stage 3 was evident in sixty-six percent of the sample by six months of age, and Stage 4 was manifested by eight months in seventy-seven percent of the babies. Yarrow emphasized in his conclusion that "a focused individualized relationship with the mother or major caretaker does not appear suddenly, but is rather a gradual development of which there are many stages."12

Bowlby's summary of the phases in the development of attachment includes: 1) Phase of Undiscriminating Social Responsiveness, and 2) Phase of Discriminating Social Responsiveness. (These are similar to Schaffer's phases.) Bowlby's third phase involves Active Initiation in Seeking Proximity and Contact. This begins at six to seven momths and continues into the third year. The phase most relevant to our interests, since it deals with the older preschooler, is Bowlby's fourth stage, The Goal-Corrected Partnership.13

This fourth stage assumes the child's ability to understand his mother's behavior (or her "set-goals," in Bowlby's terminology), with the resultant attempt on the child's part to alter his mother's plans "to fit better with his own in regard to contact, proximity, and interaction. Bowly characterized the more complex and sophisticated relationship between mother and child as a "partnership," implying an interlocking, purposive interaction important to each.

These theories about the development of attachment tie in with our own concepts of nudging, bugging and impinging, which we view as <u>messages to the child</u> regarding the caretaker's investment in him. The child's response to this caretaker-initiated behavior sets in motion a reciprocal interaction which is mutually gratifying, and hence, reinforcing.

A special aspect of the parent-child relationship involving idiosyncratic interactions and the use of pet names will be discussed in the following chapter

## NOTES

1. Bronfenbrenner, Urie, "Encounters of the Third Kind," Second Annual Lucille Austin Memorial Address, Columbia University School of Social Work, April 20, 1981 and, _____, Harvard Alumni College, June, 1978.

2. Brazelton, T. Berry, "Early Parent-Infant Reprocity" in <u>The Family: Can It Be Saved?</u> Victor Vaughan, III and T. Berry Brazelton, eds. (Year Book Medical Publishers, Inc.) 1976, pp. 131-141.

3. Lamb, Michael, <u>The Role of the Father in Child Development</u> (New York: John Wiley & Sons) 1976, p. 323.

4. Schaffer, H. Rudolph and Emerson, Peggy, "The Development of Social Attachments in Infancy," <u>Monographs of the Society for Research in Child Development,</u> Serial No. 94, Vol. 29, no. 3, 1964, p. 55.

5. Hinde, Robert, "On Describing Relationships," <u>Journal of Child Psychology and Psychiatry</u> 17 (1976): 7.

6. Ibid.

7. Ainsworth, Mary, "Attachment and Dependency,"
   pp. 100-106.

8. Bowlby, John, "The Nature of the Child's Tie to His
   Mother," International Journal of Psycho-Analysis,
   39 (1958): 350-373.

9. Schaffer, H. Rudolph, "Some Issues for Research in
   the Study of Attachment Behavior," in Determinants
   of Infant Behavior II, ed. by B. Foss (New York:
   John Wiley & Sons) 1963.

10. Ibid.

11. Yarrow, Leon, "The Development of Focused Relation-
    ships During Infancy," in The Exceptional Infant,
    Vol. 1: The Normal Infant, ed. by J. Hellmuth
    (Seattle: Special Child Publications) 1967, p. 434.

12. Ibid., p. 440.

13. These phases are reviewed and summarized in Mary
    Ainsworth, The Development of Infant-Mother Attach-
    ment," in Review of Child Development Research,
    Vol. 3, ed. Bettye Caldwell (Chicago: University of
    Chicago Press) 1973, pp. 10-13.

## Chapter Six

## PET NAMES AND IDIOSYNCRATIC INTERACTIONS

When two people have a special relationship, they often address one another in unique ways and they also may engage in playful behavior which is unique to them. This was demonstrated repeatedly in the several hours of observations of children with their parents.

This chapter describes and discusses some of these private features of attachment relationships as illustrated in the use of pet names and idiosyncratic behaviors among our study families. Since no two relationships are alike, the examples are unique. This very streak of exclusiveness suggests the presence of an attachment bond, since one would not invent a special name nor engage in an intimate interchange with someone who is unimportant.

Pet Names. Most of us who have been in love can attest to the compelling and binding quality of special nick-names or pet names between lovers. This private topic represents a special mode of communication which is common in families as well, but about which very little has been studied or written.

One of the few books on the subject of nick-names indicates that "because a name is not just a label or a mere neutral, referential device, but is rich in content and many kinds of associations, the effect of a name may last a lifetime."[1] Furthermore, our tendency to conceal family nick-names or pet names from peers the authors attribute to "tacit social knowledge" regarding the social and personality associations of names. If, in fact, "a person is named or renamed in the light of the attitudes and conceptions of others about him....then nick-names, can,....be seen as the external manifestation of the concepts of others of that individual—their implications, their biases, their limitations."[2]

In the course of five or six observation visits with each family in this study, parents' use of nick-names or pet names for their children became quite apparent. During the final visit with the families, while questioning about the child's caretaking history, we made it a practice to ask if the child had been named for anyone in particular, and if either parent had a "pet name" or a "nick-name" for him or her.

Frequently the parents initially denied the use of pet names. Usually these were revealed only when we repeated the question in a rather puzzled tone, indicating surprise that the parents did not have any special names they used for the child, "just in the family." It was this probing that induced the parents to disclose their pet names for their children. This is a private matter, not readily revealed.

Most of the pet names indicated a tender special feeling for the child, others suggested sarcasm, and some were rather neutral and asexual. We believe that the pet name often conveys the special meaning of the child to the parent, especially when it is a name exclusively used by one or both parents, and not a nickname which other caretakers also employ. The exclusiveness of use signifies a special relationship. Consider the underlying message given to the child whose mother refers to him as "My Monkey," or when the mother calls her child "Baby" or "Little Love." The resistance to sharing these private names perhaps lies in the parents' own marginal awareness of their underlying significance. The answer to Shakespeare's question, "What's in a Name?" may, in fact, be "quite a bit," especially if it is a pet name used in the privacy of the family.

Only five parents of the seventeen study children denied calling their children some special name (Cindy, Linda, Nina, Louis and Scott). Sometimes the pet names were shortened versions of the child's own name, or some play on the name, which was altered to mean something else (e.g., "Mary-Contrary"). Elizabeth's mother sometimes called Elizabeth by her name spelled backwards (e.g., Htebazile). This was a rather creative response to Elizabeth's occasional "mirror writing" (writing in which all the letters are reversed, common in some left-handed preschool children, such as Elizabeth).

Since all the children's names in this book (including Elizabeth's) are fictitious, examples of transformations which utilize the child's own name cannot be given here. However, a number of parents call their children by pet names which are not specifically derived from the child's name. Examples of these are listed in Table IX.

TABLE IX

PET NAMES USED BY MOTHERS AND FATHERS
IN REFERRING TO THE STUDY CHILDREN*

|  | Mothers | Fathers |
|---|---|---|
| BOYS | Baby | Gooker (when angry) |
|  | My Monkey | Pal |
|  | Pizza Pie | Pumpkin |
|  |  | Lamb Chop |
|  |  | Butch |
|  |  | Own Name/Boy |
|  |  | (e.g., Andy Boy) |
| GIRLS | Pumpkin | Little One |
|  | Peanut | Little Devil |
|  | Baby | Little Love |
|  | Peach |  |
|  | Pea-Pod |  |
|  | Bunky | Honey |

*Note: Nick-names and pet names were used
by twelve of the seventeen study
families. Other pet names which
are variations of the child's own
name are not reported here, since
this book uses fictitious names.

Parents may have more than one pet name for the
same child, even at a very early age, and distinctly
positive or negative moods may lead to a change of the
name. Anger toward the loved person, for example,
often leads to a withdrawal from the affectionate pet

name and a return to the more formal name,3 or the
given name may be used with extreme emphasis or form-
ality to convey disapproval (e.g., "Just what do you
think you are doing, Allison  White!:)

Two of the five study families who did not have
a pet name for their children had named their children
originally by looking through lists in a name book.
In both instances, the parents remembered and cited the
meaning of their children's given name: in one instance,
"the anointed one," and in the other, "one who is sent
to heal."

The significance of pet names rests with the meaning conveyed in the name. Again, the bottom line is
proprietary. The child belongs to and is a part of the
parent and family system in which the naming serves a
binding function. Pet names, thus, can be considered
supplemental "tags" on the family package.

Idiosyncratic Interactions. Certain behaviors such as
hugging and kissing by general consensus signify affectionate feelings. Young children learn the significance of these behaviors at an early age and they initiate such behaviors themselves from the time they can
extend their arms as a signal that they want to be
picked up and held. Kissing, hugging, lap sitting and
other such positive proximal expressions of affection
are obvious indications of the presence of meaningful
bonds.

In addition to these familiar positive expressions
of affection we were interested in discovering possible
idiosyncratic behavioral indications of attachment.
Since the use of pet names and special behaviors indicates the presence of special bonds in adult love relationships, we were alert for the possibility of uncovering analogous unique indicators of attachments in children's attachment relationships. While participation
in an idiosyncratic interaction does not automatically
indicate the presence of attachment, the instances of
such behavior which we noted during the observations
occurred much more frequently in parent-child interactions, and usually consisted of behaviors which involved proximity. It was our distinct impression that
these idiosyncratic interactions flowered and thrived
in the context of an attachment relationship and subsequently served to strengthen and perpetuate it.

104

Unique interactions occurred with the greatest
frequency in spontaneous play activities and in ritu-
alized bedtime behavior. The strong feelings of ex-
citement and pleasure which accompany these idiosyncratic interactions are very positive, and, hence,
serve to strengthen and positively reinforce the relationship.

### Idiosyncratic Interaction with Father at Bedtime
Name of Child: Paul

M and C went into C's room which was very
attractively painted and furnished in red,
white and blue. There were life-size posters
of Superman and Batman on the wall. C was
still holding the ribbon from the gift which
he told M he wanted to save. C then said to
M: "It's Daddy's turn tonight."
M called to F (who was in sib's room):
    "Your turn."
M left the room.
F came into C's room. F picked C up and
tossed him casually on his bed.
C to F: "I want you to throw me higher so
        I can fly."
F picked up C again and threw him—from some
distance—onto the bed. C laughed delightedly.
C to F: "Shake your head."
F shook his head in a vigorously playful way,
evidently part of a regular bedtime routine.
C laughed and laughed. F then kissed C and
said: "Good-night."
M then came in, kissed C and said "Good-night."

Comment: It was evident that Father's shaking
his head was part of a routine, since no explanation was requested when Paul simply
stated, "Shake your head." This habitual
behavior resembles that of Steven's father's
bedtime ritual of rocking and singing. F's
question, "Do I have to sing?" implied that
singing was the expectation.

## Idiosyncratic Interaction with Mother
Name of Child: Steven

This particular behavior was observed on
three different visits:

First, occurred during the beginning of the
dinner observation. Steven had been downstairs in his grandmother's apartment, making the dinner salad with her. M had sent
the sibling downstairs to ask C to come up.
When C came in, he saw R and seemed shy.
He went over to M and put his head in her
lap. M gently stroked his hair. After a
minute or less, C responded to a question
R asked him about school, and he lifted
his head and ran to get something to show R.

The second episode of the same type of
behavior occurred after dinner the same
evening: C was running across the living
room, and his sib put out his foot and
tripped him (deliberately). C fell and
began crying. C got up and went to M and
put his head in her lap, saying, "Jack
tripped me."

The third similar behavior was observed
during the bedtime visit: Again C was
downstairs when R arrived, watching TV
with grandmother. M called to C that it
was time to come upstairs now and get
ready for bed. C immediately began crying, and as he entered the room, he went
straight for his mother and put his head
in her lap.

Comment: This child consistently went to
his mother for comfort when he was crying
or anxious. His characteristic posture
with her (i.e., putting his head in her
lap) seemed to give him physical contact
(proximity) and soothing consolation.
Mother, in these instances, provided a
safe haven, even when she, herself, was
the source of the tears (i.e., bedtime
announcement).

106

Again, the element of routine, which gives children the structure of predictability, also serves a binding function. This became evident in verbal references to the habitual nature of some behaviors in the process of anticipating them; for example, Louis' mother's statement to him, "You always do," when she prompted him to hide from his father who was arriving home from work (example given in Chapter Five, p. 90).

For some of the very verbal children, imaginative, original bedtime stories added an exclusive quality to the joint story-telling experience, shared only between the child and that particular caretaker. We have already given the example of Elizabeth's baby-mother Hide-and-seek story game activity, which she played out with her sitter. The following example illustrates a unique, mutual story-telling bedtime interaction between Elizabeth and her father.

Idiosyncratic Interaction with Father at
Bedtime - Mutual Story Telling
Name of Child: Elizabeth

C to F:  "I want to sit on your lap."
C moved onto F's lap, and F put his arm around her.
F engaged C in pointing out items in the pictures, according to the format of the book.
After F finished the book, C said to F:
         "I want a gnome story."
F to C:  "OK, if you'll help me with it."
F to R:  "This is one we make up ourselves."
F to C:  "Remember how big gnomes are?"
C shows with two hands.
F to C:  "I thought they were smaller."
He shows with his hands."
F to C:  "And what color are their hats?"
C:       "Pink."
F:       "I thought they were red."
C to F:  "Let's pretend that we're in this house and you and Mommy are away (*ON: Again C arranges to have parents gone), and S and R are here and the gnomes come to visit."        (continued)

_____

* ON: Observational Note.

107

| | |
|---|---|
| F: | "OK, it's lunch time and you hear a knock on the door. (F knocks on the windowsill.) You go to the door and then you don't see anybody. Then you feel someone pulling on your toe (F pulls on C's toe), and you look down and you see the gnomes." |
| C to F: | "There's a Mother, Father and two children." (ON: C's family composition.) |
| F to C: | "I thought there was only one child." |
| C to F: | "No, there are two (firmly)." |
| F: | "Well, you have lunch and then you go to the pool, cause it's summer time." |
| C: | "No, it's spring." |
| F: | "I thought it was summer." |
| C: | "No, it's spring." |
| F: | "OK, will they go out on the swings?" |
| C: | "No, we're in this house" (no swings). |
| F to R: | " I haven't put up the swings yet." |
| F: | "Then you go next door to swing, and do you know how you swing? The gnomes crawl up your leg (F moves fingers up C's leg; C giggles). And then they sit on your lap and you all swing and have a good time, and that's the end of the story. Now, it's time to say good-night." |

F patted C's head.

Comment: We note the physical proximity often associated with the story-telling (i.e., the child's request to sit on father's lap, and father's putting his arm around her and using the child's body to demonstrate aspects of the story action). This physical proximity matches the feeling of psychological closeness which accompanies the sharing of a unique fantasy experience, exclusive to those two individuals.

Many mothers in our study sat or lay on their child's bed as they read to them. This was quite different from the father's bedtime behavior which usually involved having the child sit in their laps while they were sitting in a chair, either in the child's room or in the living room. Two mothers (Annalee's and Nina's) typically lie down on the bed with their daughters and

108

remain with them every evening until the child falls
asleep, having previously read to them while sitting
on the bed.

Our observation visits included one dinner visit
and one bedtime visit (separate) with every child and
family. Both of these events offer rich opportunities
for observing family interactions, thanks to the un-
abashed honesty and candid qualities of young children.
We will discuss the Family Dinner in the next chapter,
and now will focus on the Bedtime Situation, which for
the four or five-year-old child embodies the threat of
separation from the comfort and security of the family
circle, and the expectation that he or she can tolerate
a period of several hours sleeping alone in the dark.
Since many preschoolers experience this expectation as
a threat, it arouses strong feelings of stress which,
in turn, stimulates attachment reactions. Thus, bedtime is an ideal situation for studying attachment responses, including typical comforting behaviors used
to console the upset child.

Bedtime Routines. Bedtime comes at the end of a long
day for working parents and their children who have,
for the most part, been up since at least 7:00 a.m.,
and whose intervening experiences have run the gamut
from busy, to being over-stimulated, to being exhausted.
The working mother of a preschool child frequently has
a lot of responsibilities for household chores, even in
families in which the fathers share in the child care.
One of the mothers (Louis'), obviously tired as she sat
on her child's bed preparing to read him a bedtime story,
sighed deeply and said, "I really feel beat today—
sometimes I think I'm too old to have a kid this age"
(mother was 36). Later this mother stated her belief
that she probably spends more time playing with her
young child than do some of the non-working mothers in
the neighborhood. She may have been correct in spite
of the defensiveness in her explanation.

The example is given to set the tone for the bedtime experience. Both parents and children are usually
very tired, and some of the parents are consciously
aware of wanting to get the child in bed and asleep so
that they can have some time for themselves. This was
reflected in parting bedtime comments such as the following:

109

Matthew's mother:    "Goodnight.  Don't get up,
                      and try not to wet your
                      bed," and
Elizabeth's mother, who told the child she
could color by herself, then,
                      "Turn off your light, and
                      don't scream."

Steven's mother, who was very surprised to learn
one evening that the researcher was going to visit
another child at 9:00 p.m., admitted to being very
eager to get her children into bed by 8:00 p.m.  She
said furthermore that she gets very angry if the children get up after they have been put to bed.

M to R:    "I'm tired at night, and I don't
            want to keep going back to them.
            I need some time to myself.  Just
            like when I pick them up at school
            and bring them home.  I need a few
            minutes to myself to change my clothes
            and put my feet up.  Sometimes the
            kids start climbing all over me and
            I tell them, 'I need a few minutes
            to myself, then I'll take you to
            the pool.'"

Other examples could be given illustrating the
strain of fatigue on the working mother and their
diverse coping adaptations to this.  The fathers in
this study seemed less prone to irritability that was
obvious during the end-of-the-day observations.

The parents of some of the only children (Nina,
Annalee, and Walter) seemed less anxious about getting
them to bed.  These parents frequently included their
children in various activities which might, in other
families, tend to be shared by the mother and father
alone.

Approximately seven of the seventeen study children appeared to have some form of bedtime problem as
reported by the parents, or as observed during the
visits (Annalee, Nina, Cindy, Matthew, Kathy, Steven
and Kim).  Some examples follow.

Cindy sleeps with her older sibling in a
double bed; she claimed to be looking for-
ward to having a room of her own after the
family moved to a new house in a few months.

Cindy pouted and fussed about going to bed
during the researcher's last visit. Her
mother had told her that Mrs. Webb was coming to see how good she goes to bed, and
the child had responded: "But I don't go
to bed good!"

The most severe bedtime problem was demonstrated
by Kim, who cried and fussed until her mother let her
have her way during our observation visit (she wanted
to join her older sister in the sister's bed). In this
family it was the practice for the children to put on
clean clothes at night after their baths. They slept
in their day clothing in order to save time in the
morning. The mother had told us about this during the
first visit during the filling out of the questionnaire,
and we observed the behavior during the bedtime visit.
The excerpt which follows describes the bedtime interaction between Kim and her mother:

Example: Bedtime Interaction
Name of Child: Kim

M to C:   "Look at the clock and tell me
          what time it is."
C said nothing.
M to C:   "It's after nine o'clock—it's
          time for bed."
C to M:   (in a very loud voice)
          "I don't want to go to bed."
M to C:   "Well, you have to."
C to M:   "I want to sleep with Laurie."
          (sibling)
M to C:   "No, you're going to sleep in
          your own bed tonight."
M then proceeded to take sibling (age seven)
to her room, where there was a brief period
of crying. Meanwhile C had disappeared. When
M returned she asked R where C was, then said:
          "She's probably hiding."

111

M and R went into the living room where C
had crawled under a chair.
M to C:  "Come on out."
C to M:  "No!  I want to sleep with Laurie."
M to C:  "Well, then come out."
C came out and M picked her up.  C began
crying.
M told C to say "Good-bye" to R.  M took C
into C's room, where a favorite afghan had
been arranged on top of the bed.  M left
the room, saying:
          "Now you stay there."
C was still calling out:
          "I want to sleep with Laurie."
M to C:  "Will you sleep?"
C to M:  "Yes."
M to C:  "Well, OK."
C ran down hall to sibling's bedroom.  M
followed her, then came back a few minutes
later to the kitchen where R was waiting.
C to M:  "You come and sleep with us."
M to C:  "I will later.  I'm talking to
          Mrs. Webb now."
F, who had come home late from work, appeared
at the door.
M to F:  "I'm letting them sleep together.
          You'd better go kiss them goodnight."

Comment:  After a day separated from her
mother and sister, this child seemed to
want family members with her at night
time.  Kim's bedtime doll play story had
ended with the whole family together in
the same bed.

Bedtime problems in one form or another are fairly
common among preschool children, and we certainly do
not suggest that those reported here would not exist
if the mothers were not working.  There seemed to be
no correlation among this group of children between
the age of the child when the mother went to work and
the incidence of "problems."

In some families there appeared to be very good
feelings generated in the bedtime behavior, and in a
few it was taken very much for granted.  In all seventeen families observed except one (Elizabeth's) a bedtime kiss by one or both parents seemed to be part of

the ritual. An interval of story reading or story inventing preceded the bedtime in twelve of the families. This seemed to relax the child, provided a period of physical closeness between the child and the parent, and also offered a time for mutual concentration on a shared activity.

We have noted several examples of the young child's attempt to maintain proximity with attachment figures to avoid the separation stress implicit in the bedtime experience. Routinized affectionate and comforting behaviors are common at bedtime, as evident in lap-sitting and goodnight kisses. Idiosyncratic and routinized behaviors and parents' use of pet names with their children lend a very special quality to the interaction, one which tends to reinforce the attachment bond.

## NOTES

1. Morgan, Jane, O'Neill, Christopher and Harre', Rom, Nicknames: Their Origins and Social Consequences (London: Routledge & Kegan Paul) 1979, p. 10.

2. Ibid., p. 105-106.

3. Ibid., p. 31.

Chapter Seven

# THE INVISIBLE UMBILICAL OF FAMILY BONDS

The nine month period prior to the birth of a child is pregnant with meaning for the entire kinship group which surround the mother and father. They plan, discuss, and sometimes worry about the impact of the new addition to their family circle. The preparations and expectations, hopes and dreams, initiate the parent-to-child bonding process long before the parents see their baby. Whether the baby's conception was planned or unplanned, by the time of the actual birth the parents have created certain ideas about the child, which subsequently become woven into their attachment feelings toward the infant.

After the baby's birth the dreams become reality and the parent's bonding behavior takes the form of fondling, kissing, cuddling, and prolonged gazing at the infant. These behaviors are tangible expressions of the psychological attachment. Klaus and Kennel[1] have stressed the importance of tactile and visual early contact for bonding between baby and mother. This is especially important in situations of premature births which often results in long periods of mother-child separation. They believe that "failure to thrive" without organic cause, as well as incidences of infant battering are significantly related to early separation of mothers and babies at or near birth, with resulting absence of the usual bonding process.[2]

The notion of a "critical period" for bonding has been questioned by some researchers,[3] but regardless of the issue of timing (whether it must occur immediately after birth), we know that the child needs repeated contact with someone who cares very much about him or her in order to grow and develop normally.

The importance of the child to the parent is thus a vital prelude to the development of the child's reciprocal attachment, which emerges gradually in the course of the baby's first year of life. Long before the baby's actual birth—perhaps even before its conception—the parent has invested that child with special meaning.[4] The impact of prenatal expectations is confirmed by the mourning process which typically

115

accompanies the birth of a defective child. This requires that parents give up their unrealized image of the anticipated "normal" child, before they can establish a meaningful relationship with the actual "defective" infant who has been born to them.[5]

Parents influence their children both directly and indirectly. We believe that much of parental impingement on children, expressed through socialization efforts, represents the (often unconscious) intent of the parent to convert the real child into the anticipated image of their prenatal attachment fantasized child.

A child growing up in a particular family has varied expectations to meet. The family communicates these via subtle, non-verbal, as well as verbal, messages. The umbilical cord of family bonds continually tugs and restrains the growing child in a manner which makes him or her very aware of the power and influence of the parents whose grip on the reins keeps the child securely within the confines of family influence. The child's gradual awareness of his importance to parents and kin fosters his own attachment to them. A growing sense of the concept of the family as a unit also develops gradually, accompanying the spreading of attachment bonds to various family members.

The Family Dinner. Bowlby considers attachment an innate behavior, not dependent on need satisfaction for its development.[6] However, the early feeding situation in which the caretaker cradles the child in her (or his) arms, and maintains steady eye contact while the infant suckles contentedly presents a prototype of bonding in which the feeding process is a central, if not essential, component. In everyday parlance, food equals love, a truism which puts the family dinner into perspective as the site of both physiological and psychological nurturance.

Our study of attachment included the family dinner observation as an important arena for studying critical interactions among family members. Traditionally, according to Stephen White, the family meal has been

> a stable ritual (where) children learn the rules of family life, etiquette, religious observance, bodily functions, sensuous enjoyment and the expression of feelings.[7]

116

When both parents work, and the family has been separated all day, the dinner meal represents a kind of reunion to which the various members come with diverse needs and expectations. The irony is that although the expectations and intentions of family members may be clear, fatigue and the pressure of time may ultimately interfere with the desired satisfaction of either physical or emotional needs.

Many study parents referred to the dinner meal as "a very hectic time." Children and parents are usually tired at the end of the day, and reserves of tact may be low. Some parents respond to this stress by permissiveness, "to avoid hassles," while others find the child's finicky eating or poor manners "the last straw," and irritability becomes evident. The following example illustrates a compromise motivated by the reality of fatigue:

> Annalee's mother lets the child eat by herself if she is hungry before the father arrives home from work. She also lets C choose what she wants for dinner. M to R:  "I don't want to make her and my life difficult on the days we both are tired.  On weekends we are all together and we eat together, but on weekdays I don't insist."

Jules Henry in his study of family relationships stated that "food and mealtimes (may activate) underlying tensions: people (can) use food and mealtime against one another."[8]  Among the study families, tensions often seemed to take the form of coaxing the child to eat, criticizing the child's table manners or bickering about the dessert.  Since we assumed that the families made some effort to appear at their best during our visit, it is likely that overt expressions of tension occurred with _greater_ frequency than we observed.

Our procedure for observing the dinner involved sitting at the table with the family and usually having coffee or a cold soft drink while the family had their evening meal.  In every instance when the meal was announced and the family gathered at the table, if the researcher was not told where to sit she always asked where the parents wanted her to sit.  As the family

took their seats the researcher asked if they usually
sat in particular locations, and if they were in their
"regular seats" now. The researcher wanted to avoid
sitting in any family member's "regular seat." Dia-
grams of the seating arrangements were included in the
researcher's notes (completed after the observations).

Review of the field notes reveals that in only
seven of the eighteen meals observed was the mealtime experience without observable stress. Coaxing to
eat, as described in the example of Scott, below, was
very common ("excessive" in five families, and present
in a lesser degree in two others). Threats to send the
child from the table if he or she didn't "behave" were
made in four families, with one threat actually carried
out. Crying at the table, with children subsequently
leaving and returning, occurred in two instances. Almost without exception it was the mother who assumed the
coaxing and/or disciplinary role during dinner. In
four families (Scott's Anna's, Paul's and Walter's),
the father chimed in and backed mother up—however,
the threats to exclude the child from the table in-
variably came from the mother.

> Example: Family Dinner Interaction
> Name of Child: Scott
>
> Sibling had finished her meal and had left
> the table. She went into her room (visible
> from the kitchen) and lay down on her bed
> with a book. C was not eating much at all.
> M and F in turn kept prompting him to finish.
> This continued for at least five minutes.
> C said: "I'm ready for a doughnut now,"
> (dessert R had brought).
> M to C: "You have to eat some more first."
>
> Comment: Scott's parents claim to be very
> flexible about bedtime, naps and meal times
> since they believe that "children should be
> allowed leeway to do these things when they
> want to, rather than according to a rigid
> schedule." These permissive values, however,
> were not evident in their behavior during
> this observation.

The dinner observation was our second visit to
the family home, and typically followed an observation

of the child in the day care setting. Since we wondered if some of the strained behavior might be due to
anxiety about our presence, we made it a practice to
ask the parents at some point before leaving whether
the child's behavior during the visit had been typical,
or whether they thought things were different, due to
having a stranger present. Except for Annalee's
mother who thought the child was "more silly" during
our visit, the rest of the families said that the
child's behavior was, indeed, commonplace. A few
mothers spontaneously, as if looking for sympathy,
said directly to us during the disturbing episode:
"Unfortunately, we go through this almost _every_ night!"

A review of the families where the meal was _not_
a source of conflict (Nina, James, Linda, Elizabeth,
Matthew, Ronald and Kim) revealed that the children
in this group were somewhat older on the average than
those whose parents coaxed or became annoyed. Perhaps
appetites and manners improve with age along with increased skillfulness on the part of both parent and
children in dealing with one another!

Some examples follow:

Examples:  Family Dinner Interactions

Name of Child:  Louis

M put spaghetti and salad on the table and
began serving as she mentioned C's upcom-
ing birthday party.  C began eating the
meatballs and said to M:
          "I don't want spaghetti."
M to R:   "He's already eaten two bananas
          since coming home from school.
          He's big on fruit."
C began eating an apple and seemed to become
increasingly more excited (not clear why).
He stood up on his chair.
M to C:   "You sit down."
C to M:   (mockingly)  "You sit down."
          C laughed.
C to M:   "My face is laughing."
M to C:   "Your tushy won't be laughing in
          a minute."
M slapped C on bottom.  C sat down, (did
not cry).

119

C did not like the chicken which was offered
her, wanting "the red kind" being served to
others.
M to C: "You never liked the red kind before."
C to M: "I do too. I want it."
M to C: "You're thinking of a different kind.
I don't have that."
C to M: "I want some of that" (pointing to
red chicken).
M gave it to her.
After everyone was served, M said to C:
"Are you going to say Grace, Kathy?"
C shook her head No.
R to C: "Do you know how to say Grace?"
F to R: "She says it very well."
M coaxed once again.
C shook her head and M said to F:
"You say it."
F did so.

Later, C asked M if she could have dessert;
she wanted to get doughnuts R had brought.
F was clearing the table. M told C she could
get one. In kitchen F evidently had opened
the box and C had wanted to do it. C screamed
to F: "I can do it!"
F to C: "You can do it, but you may not
do it."
C began crying as F returned to the table.
M explained to F that she had given C permis-
sion to get a doughnut.
F (calling to C who was still crying in the
kitchen): "I didn't know Mommy told you you
could get one. I'm sorry. Come
join us with your doughnut."
C came back to the table and climbed into M's
lap where she sat eating her doughnut.

Comment: This brief excerpt demonstrates how
this child has learned to withhold, as a way
of exerting power over her parents. She was
coaxed to do, to tell, and to show as much
(or more than) any other child in the study,
except possibly Lori. The child's oppositional behavior is perhaps a reaction to what
may be experienced by her as too much unsolicited impinging. There is a circular effect

to the coaxing, moreover, which seems to
increase as the child repeatedly refuses
to comply with parents' requests.

The following example also illustrates the behavior of a controlling child—yet her manner of controlling her father is witty and engaging, resulting
in a happy and stimulating interchange for the whole
family.

<u>Name of Child</u>:  Linda

C ate a lot and wanted more especially
the marrow bones of the lamb chops.  At
one point in the meal C asked F:
    "Do you like vegetables, Daddy?"
F did not respond because sibling was agi-
tating about being driven to his Little
League game.  F and sib left. When F returned (five minutes later) he went to
the freezer and asked,
    "What's a paper tent doing in
    the freezer?"
(This was a Father's Day gift of peanut
brittle which Linda made that day at
school.)
C to F:  (smiling with glee) "It's for
        you, but you can't have it until
        tomorrow, and you have to guess
        what it is first."
A ten-minute guessing game followed with
F finally saying to C:
    "Tell me what letter it starts with."
C to F:  "K" (for candy).  There were peals
        of laughter over this as M explained
        to C how to spell candy.

In summary, we consider the Family Dinner as a
rich setting for observations of the dynamic interactions between the child and various family members.
In eleven out of eighteen families there was observable
stress connected with the child's eating.  The mother
tended to assume the role of disciplinarian, sometimes
backed up by the father.  Threats to exclude the child
from the table occurred in several families.  In families where the meal was not stressful, the children
tended to be older, on the average.

In retrospect, it would have been very interesting to have observed these children during a meal with their parents absent. Our impression was that the tension and conflict originated in the parent-child (especially mother-child) relationship, and our guess is that these same children would not have become involved in similar meal time conflicts in the presence of other caretakers. Again, the mother's active involvement in impinging behaviors, suggests to us her strong attachment to the child which precipitates her self-ascribed persistent role as disciplinarian and socializing agent.

Significance of Family Bonds. Our thesis is that there is "something very special" about the parent-child relationships, not present in other caretaking relationships, and that this "special component" emanates from the parent's strong attachment to the child. The parent's impinging behaviors, use of pet names and idiosyncratic play and comforting activities encourage and support the child's reciprocal attachment to the parent.

Grandparents, also, become significant secondary attachment figures for the child, even in the face of relatively little interaction with them, since the child senses his or her importance to the grandparent. We believe this is the bottom line for attachment formation: the sense that one has great significance to someone else. This would explain the child's selection of the grandparent as most preferred sitter on the questionnaires, in spite of the dearth of grandparent-initiated activities with the child, compared to the high degree of activity with teen-age, unrelated sitters. It is noteworthy also that grandparents frequently use pet names with their grandchildren, whereas unrelated sitters rarely did.

This key principle of the sense of one's own significance to another as essential for attachment throws new light on the whole issue of relationships with teachers and unrelated sitters as possibly compromising the basic parent-child attachment. We view attachment as not based upon the amount of time two people spend together, but rather on the underlying meaning of the relationship itself which confers special importance to any shared activity, even if very time-limited.

From this point of view, the negative attention and stress caused by mother's nudging and bugging at

dinner is essentially reassuring to the four-year-old
who has spent all day competing with ten or eleven
peers for a comment or a smile from the day care teacher. In essence, the child knows he or she is very important to the parents and grandparents, and this knowledge is an essential nutrient for the child's emotional well-being.

Our view of attachment even helps us understand
the reason why children who are battered usually re-
tain a sense of attachment to the abusing parent. The
children realize that they are, in fact, important to
that parent, and this conviction overrides the painful
experiences of abuse and stand as sad confirmation of
the fact that even negative attention is better than no
attention.

Absence of this sense of one's importance to the
parents, and/or other caretaking kin, can lead to "non-
attachment," which we maintain flows from an essential
flaw in the basic parent-to-child bonding experience,
rather than from unstable, poor quality child care as
implied in Fraiberg's position.[9] Undesirable as unstable care is for children, we regard it as a separate
issue from that of the basic parent-child attachment
relationship.

Family bonds are powerful and enduring ties. The
parents'and relatives' feelings about the child serve
as the nutritive soil for the growth of a healthy seed-
ling.

We will now look at the children's perceptions of
their families, as expressed in their drawings, stories
and in their spontaneous conversations with non-parental
caretakers.

The Children's Views of Their Families. The projective
story completion doll play interviews were an integral
part of the study design. We have already discussed
our reasons for using this particular technique as a
means of involving the child in an interview which has
intrinsic appeal to preschoolers. We have also given
numerous examples of the children's verbatim stories
to illustrate our theoretical discussion of attachment
from the children's vantage point.

In the course of working with the children we
added an additional projective technique  to enrich

our study of children's views of their families. This procedure, which we called the "Draw-a-Family" technique, simply involves providing the child with crayons and drawing paper, and then asking him or her to draw a family. We encouraged the child to talk as he or she was drawing, and we made notes of the child's comments, which we later attached to the drawing itself.

The children's own identification with their family drawings was openly admitted by most children as they volunteered that they were drawing specific family member's eyes and hair the same colors as those of their own respective family members. This identification was similar to spontaneous statements many children made during the projective stories, such as, "She (doll) is a sister, because I'm a sister of a brother," and "Her (doll's) room is upstairs, like mine is." The children consistently desired to have the story characters conform to the child's own family structure, and many children who did not have regular contact with their grandparents eliminated these older doll figures early in the play episodes.

We analyzed the Draw-a-Family sketches according to the following questions:

Which family member is drawn the largest?
Which family member is drawn with most detail?
Which family members are in closest proximity to the study child?

The importance of relative size of different family members is emphasized by Joseph DiLeo, a psychiatrist who has written about the interpretation of children's drawings. DeLeo states: "Like the ancient Egyptians, the young child....uses size to express the importance attributed to a person, (and) the awe and esteem in which that person is held."[10]

In regard to relative position, DiLeo indicates that "the child will tend to place himself next to the favored parent."[11] DiLeo summarizes:

Children's drawings of the family
are valuable expressions of their
feelings and how they view the
transactional patterns within the
family.... The family drawing can

124

be viewed as an unstructured projective technique that may reveal
the child's feelings in relation
to those whom he regards as most
important and whose formative influence is most powerful.[12]

The drawings were evaluated and coded by two independent judges in terms of the three questions (above),
and then an "attachment choice" was determined for each
child. The form for summarizing this data is in the
Appendix.

For children whose manual dexterity and interest
revealed minimal drawing skills, this technique was a
simple and effective way of uncovering spontaneous feelings about family members, in addition to gathering further information regarding attachment preferences.

There was, however, quite extensive variation in
drawing ability among our sample, presumably because
of different degrees of small muscle development. Four
children did not wish to attempt the family drawing,
with two saying clearly that it was "too hard" for them
to do so. This was not strictly a matter of age, since
Lori, the youngest child in our study, managed to complete a very respectable drawing, which she then stead-
fastly refused to give us.

The children who became involved in this activity
usually drew their own family portraits, even though
this was not the specific request. Sometimes the family
pet was included, and sometimes the children would become concerned if they ran out of space on the paper so
that all the members of their family could not be included. Often the child's spontaneous comments about
him or herself, or about family members, proved to be
quite revealing as the child worked to convey the details of his or her perceived reality.

Examples: Child's Family Drawing

Name of Child: James

R said she would like to see how C draws.
Would he draw a picture of a family for
her to keep?
C to R: "Yes."
C sat at F's desk and began by drawing sun,
grass, and the dog. He held it up and named
what he had done.

125

M to C:  "That's good."
C:       "Who should I make next?  I
         guess I'll make myself."
After himself, C drew F (very tall), then
M.  He then became disturbed because he had
no more room for his brother.  R suggested
that he had room over the dog.
F to R:  "He never puts any arms on the
         people."
(Actually C did put arms on his <u>own</u> figure,
but not on any of the other family members.)
C:       "I have sandy color hair.  What
         color should I use?"
Brother: "Mix yellow and brown."
C did so.
He then proceeded to draw other family mem-
bers with accurate hair color.  At end C
held up picture and smiled.
R asked him to put his name on it.  He did
so on the back saying,
         "I hate the name James, but I like
         my middle name."
C printed his entire name on the drawing.


## Name of Child:  Scott

R to C:  "I brought crayons and paper today
         because I want to see you draw a
         picture."
M to R:  "I was so pleased when C began
         drawing forms this year."
R to C:  "Would you draw a picture of a
         family for me to keep?"
C to R:  "Yes."
C drew sibling first, then a flower, then
himself, then F with a lot of hair (head
only, no body), then the M (also only the
head).  As C drew M's hair he said:
         "It's a witch."
(M winced as C said this.)
Then as he drew the mouth, C said,
         "She's smiling."

Name of Child: Ronald
(Note:   Recall that C has twin brothers,
         eighteen months younger than him-
         self.)

R put out paper and crayons after dinner
and C and one sibling began drawing.  C
drew three figures, all exactly alike, all
with the same color—blue.
C:           "They're wearing their blue suits."
M to C:      "They all have heads, bodies, legs
             and feet.  What else do they need?"
             (no arms were visible)
C added a dot to each foot to represent the
toe.

In retrospect it would have been interesting to
have asked the child to make up a story about the family after the drawing was complete.

Preschool children are good observers of detail
regarding physical attributes, and the drawings reflected their attempts to convey their observations
with as much accuracy as possible.

Using the tally sheets conforming to DiLeo's
interpretations regarding the meaning of children's
drawings, we found that there was extreme variability
in the detail and size with which children drew family
members.

Among the fifteen of the original sample of nineteen children who completed family drawings, the father
figured predominately in five sketches, and the mother
in two.  Mother and father seemed to share equal bill-
ing in the drawings of two other children, while an
additional two gave equal preference to all family
figures.  Still further variations revealed two children as most involved with the portrayals of their siblings, and two others being very interested in their
own self-portraits.

Our attempt to derive an "attachment preference"
based on evaluation of the children's family drawings
needs more refinement.  Analysis of the drawings alone
seems insufficient without reference to the children's
accompanying verbalizations.  We regard the child's

127

"Draw-a-Family" projective technique as an adjunct to the projective stories, as a method for eliciting attachment preferences. We also recognize that this technique (instrument) is not as intrinsically appealing as is the doll play interview to the average four-year-old child. However, for those to whom it does appeal, it can add appreciably to the child's portrayal of his or her family situation.

The thoughts of the preschool child are very family oriented. Even when they spend fewer hours per week in their family home than elsewhere, and less time with their parents than with non-related caretakers, their conversations are sprinkled liberally with references to mothers, fathers, and siblings. The child in day care will say, "Hang it up so my Mommy can see it," or "My Daddy likes to watch baseball on TV." Identification with the same sex parent is developing during this period and is very evident in comments such as "I'm going to be a Boy Scout, like my Daddy" (Paul), and "I curled my hair and have on eye shadow, like Mommy" (Kim).

Many young children of working parents have already experienced an array of sitters and different child care arrangements. The constant factor in their lives is that Mother and Father remain the same, and the child who senses his or her own significance to these people, naturally valorizes the relationship with them. Parental relationships and those involving relatives last for life, and even a young child with an immature perception of time must be aware that although sitters and teachers come and go, the all-important Mommy, Daddy, Gramma and Grampa not only keep coming back, but when they do they are intensely involved and interested in him or her. Attachments within the context of the family circle thus are crucial and compelling bonds of self-affirmation and security for the preschool child.

NOTES

1. Klaus, Marshall and Kennell, John, Maternal-Infant Bonding (St. Louis: The C.V. Mosby Co.) 1976, pp. 1-15.

2. Ibid.

3. Shapiro, Theodore, Discussion:  "Problems of Mother-Infant Bonding," Conference on Contemporary Issues in Child Mental Health Practice, New York Foundling Hospital, New York, June 3, 1981.

4. Ibid.

5. Solnit, Alfred J. and Stark, M. H., "Mourning and the Birth of a Defective Child, "Psychoanalytic Study of the Child, 16, 1961: 523-537.

6. Bowlby, op. cit.

7. White, Stephen L., "Family Dinner Time: A Focus for Gathering Family History" (Master's thesis, Smith College School for Social Work, Northampton, Mass.) 1974, p. 9.

8. Henry, Jules, Pathways to Madness (New York: Random House) 1971, p. 452.

9. Fraiberg, op. cit., pp. 45-62.

10. DiLeo, Joseph, Children's Drawings as Diagnostic Aids (New York: Brunner/Mazel) 1973, p. 113.

11. Ibid., p. 112.

12. Ibid., p. 100.

# IV    ADVANTAGES OF

## MULTIPLE CARETAKING EXPERIENCES

# IV ADVANTAGES OF MULTIPLE CARETAKING EXPERIENCES

Childrearing practices and philosophies change over time, reflecting prevailing cultural values, social mores, and economic conditions. Many of our grandparents at the turn of the century believed sincerely, for example, that if they spared the rod, their children (our parents) would be spoiled. These very children may have subsequently raised <u>their</u> children in a much less authoritarian mode, with some, perhaps, moving toward a permissive extreme in regard to discipline. Today, the psychologically sophisiticated parent may understand and support the child's need to develop an internalized super-ego and a sense of self-esteem as the foundation for self-motivated acceptable behavior.

Human nature is very adaptable; the young child, ignorant of how his grandmother took care of his mother, adjusts to whatever type of care he receives. The parents, by contrast, with their broader knowledge of child care options may wonder and worry about whether the type of care they are providing for their child is beneficial or harmful.

This is particularly true regarding the issue of using multiple caretakers. Most working parents have no choice but to arrange alternate care for their children. Many who do this out of necessity, believe that it would be better if they remained home as their child's principal caretaker. Two mothers in this study felt this way, and spontaneously connected their motivation for participating in this research to their concern about the possible emotional consequences of their work-related absences on their child. They had searched in their local libraries for an objective discussion to help them deal with their own conflicted views on this subject.

The discussion in the next two chapters emphasizes the <u>advantages</u> of multiple caretaking experiences for young children, since the <u>disadvantages</u> have been clearly stated by Fraiberg and others,[1] and are generally uppermost in the minds of most working parents. We do not pretend that there are no disadvantages. Rather, we think the advantages are far less evident since they have been generally ignored or glossed over, and we believe it is important and timely for parents to consider some of the potential benefits to the child who receives multiple care.

The consensus of the research to date shows <u>no</u> evidence of substantial social or emotional problems due to mother's working and concomitant use of multiple caretaking, including day care.[2] However, this should not be construed as a blanket endorsement of day care or even of multiple caretaking as Rutter's (1981) comprehensive overview (including ninety-two citations) of "The Social-Emotional Consequences of Day Care for Preschool Children" indicates. Many qualifying conditions must be considered, such as lack of longitudinal studies, the influence of the <u>type</u>, and quality, and stability of care received, and also the important variable of the mother's attitude about working.

Thus, we come full circle to the mother's (and, inevitably, also father's) attitudes and feelings about their lives, and the impact of the parents' feelings and decisions on their young children. Since the importance of the mother's attitude about working inevitably filters down to the child, and many studies attest to the importance of this critical variable on the child's adjustment, our intent is to present the experience of multiple caretaking in terms of the positive effects this can bring to the child. Our hope is that if educators and mental health professionals are aware of the potential advantages in multiple caretaking, they will communicate these to parents. Then the parents' greater comfort with their decisions about child care ultimately will accrue beneficially to the children.

We do not wish to imply that "kids can survive anything," and that arrangements should not be selected and monitored with utmost care. Our guidance to parents is, however, that once having made "the best possible arrangements under the circumstances," it is fruitless, and probably counter-productive to worry and obsess over the decision in terms of its impact on the child.

Mindful, also, of the unique and singular power of their attachment relationship with their child, as discussed in Chapter Seven, parents should not fear that their parental influence will become usurped by others, since the truth is that no one can really ever take their place in their children's lives.

In recent years there has been much discussion in
the popular literature about the amount of time parents
spend with their children vis. a vis. the so-called
"quality" of the interaction.  The assumption is that
some parent-child activities are intrinsically more
worthwhile than others.  The implication also is that
mothers who stay home with their children automatically
engage them in valuable experiences, and that mothers
who work outside the home need to make a conscious
effort to choose carefully how to spend their few, very
precious hours with their children.

Mary Jo Bane states that

> there is some evidence that
> working mothers especially in
> the middle class try to make
> up for their working by set-
> ting aside time for exclusive
> attention to their children.
> They probably read more to
> their children and spend more
> time in planned activities with
> them than do non-working mothers.[4]

This would be an apt description of many of the
mothers in this study, who certainly would be interested in another quote from Bane:

> There is no evidence as to how
> much time mothers a century ago
> spent with their children.  Un-
> doubtedly, it was less than con-
> temporary non-working mothers,
> since mothers of a century ago
> had more children and probably
> also had more time-consuming
> household tasks.[5]

Studies of contemporary "non-working" mothers indicate that even women who are home all the time with
their children only spend about 1.4 hours per day on
child care.[6]

Most parents are strongly motivated to "do well" in their parenting role, even as they set goals for themselves in the workplace. Many, however, compare the situation of their own childhood with the experience of their children today, without adequately taking account of the totally different social environment of today's world. Probably few of today's parents were themselves cared for in institutionalized programs and by non-related caretakers. Parents, thus, cannot identify with their children's caretaking experiences, and they therefore approach the situation with understandable apprehension. A close look at what their young children stand to gain from the unique opportunity of relating to a diversity of caretakers may help put this' unknown into clearer perspective.

## NOTES

1. Fraiberg, Selma, Every Child's Birthright: In Defense of Mothering (New York: Basic Books) 1977, and
   Salk, Lee, Preparing for Parenthood (New York: David McKay) 1974.

2. See, Rutter, Michael, American Journal of Orthopsychiatry, 51:1, January 1981, pp. 4-28, and Michael Lamb, "Maternal Employment and Child Development" in M. E. Lamb (ed.) Nontraditional Families: Parenting and Child Development, (Hillsdale, N.J.: L. Erlbaum Assoc.) 1982, pp. 45-70.

3. See, especially, Yarrow, Marion, et. a. "Child rearing in families of working and non-working mothers," Sociometry 25, 1962, pp. 122-140, and Hoffman, Lois, "Effects of Maternal Employment on the Child—A Review of the Research," Developmental Psychology, 10, 1974, pp. 204-228.

4. Bane, Mary Jo, Here to Stay: American Families in the Twentiety Century (New York: Basic Books) 1976, p. 17.

5. Ibid., p. 16.

6. Survey Research Center, "Summary of United States Time Use Summary," Mimeo, (Ann Arbor, Michigan, University of Michigan) 1966.

Chapter Eight

## EXTENDING THE SECURITY NETWORK

The human life cycle is a responsive process, sensitive to the opportunities, limitations and expectations of the physical and social environment surrounding it. Both ends of the developmental spectrum are currently undergoing drastic change. On the one end, medical expertise and improved living conditions are expanding life expectancy far beyond what it was two decades ago. And on the other end, children are moving out of their homes at progressively younger ages for the purpose of receiving care when their parents cannot provide it at home. Not only can children growing up today anticipate a much longer life span than that of their parents, in all likelihood much of this life will be shared with a wider social network. Certainly, the years of early childhood, the so-called "formative" years, will reflect the influence on the child of numerous adults, in addition to the mother and father.

Today's three-year-olds routinely confront experiences previously reserved for children twice their age. Lois Murphy's wonderful book title, The Widening World of Childhood,[1] conveys the idea of the gradual opening up of social contacts as the child grows older. For many children of working parents the world of childhood includes extensive contact with the wide world beyond the family from infancy on. School entry, which for our grandparents began with First Grade at age six, now occurs for most children with kindergarten at age five, and for hundreds of thousands of children of working parents, with full-time day care at age three. It is ironic that the half-day kindergarten program, conceived as a gradual introduction to formal schooling, now for many children follows two years of full-time experience in day-long group programs. In fact, the very term "preschool" is really a misnomer for three to five-year-olds, when we consider that many children and families refer to day care and nursery programs as "school," and to their caretakers there as "teachers."

The idea of the shrinking world of childhood recognizes with Christopher Lasch[2] that children are being exposed to more stimulating and diverse experiences at increasingly younger ages. A 1981 New York Times magazine article asked, "Whatever Became of Childhood Innocence?"[3] The social historians can answer this

137

question with the perspective of several hundred years, and the knowledge that childhood itself is a relative concept that has only been with us since the seventeenth century.[4] Prior to that time children were not treated as distinct from adults, but wore smaller size adult clothing and were expected to work to contribute to the family's economic well-being. Furthermore they were privy to adult jokes, conversations and behavior, even when this was sexually explicit.

The twentieth century reformers, having "discovered" childhood, then proceeded to try to protect it with child labor laws, compulsory schooling, and attitudes which, largely because of Freud and his followers, placed great emphasis on the importance of the first five years of life. Generational distinctions became more pronounced as recognition of the child's extreme economic and psychological dependence on the parents served to accentuate the critical role and function of parenthood.

It may be that we are currently in the midst of another social change in the way we view and treat young people between the ages of birth to five years. Working parents who must entrust their young children to out-of-home caretakers want their children to accept these arrangements. They appreciate, valorize and implicitly and explicitly reward the child who is "relatively independent" and who accepts the substitute caretakers the parents provide in their absence. While we will never return to seventeenth century mores and treat children as miniature adults, a compromise of sorts seems to be evolving, since total and extreme dependence of the child on the parents is now neither appropriate nor necessary.

This should not be interpreted as a negation of the young child's basic needs for nurturance, love and protection. It is rather a recognition of the malleability of human nature and a warning against rigid adherence to "the old ways as the best ways." There are, in fact, many ways to rear healthy, happy children, and using many caretakers is one of them.

The discussion which follows will first establish a theoretical foundation for the concept of multiple attachments and then move into a consideration of the move toward independence as illustrated in the lives of our study children. We will then consider the critical issue of separation as this applies to the timing of mother's return to work or school vis. a vis. the child's "readiness" to adapt to other caretakers.

Multiple Caretakers/Multiple Attachments. Virtually all researchers from Bowlby on who have studied attachment formation attest to the existence of multiple attachments in most children by twelve to eighteen months of age. The area which is less clear has to do with the sequence leading up to the eventual multiattached state. Some researchers (Kotelchuck,[5] Lamb[6]) have found that attachments to fathers parallel, rather than follow those to mothers. Other studies (Schaffer and Emerson,[7] Yarrow[8]) indicate that maternal attachment usually preceeds attachments to fathers and other family members.

Schaffer and Emerson found that by eighteen months of age almost one-third of the children in their sample had five or more attachment objects (i.e., people). They believe that "whom an infant chooses as his attachment object, and how many objects he selects depends primarily on the nature of the social setting in which he is reared and not on some intrinsic characteristic of the attachment function itself."[9] According to these authors

> There appears to be no inherent mechanism in the infant which insists that initially attachments must be formed to one person only. This depends entirely on the learning opportunities held out to the infant in his particular social environment. In most cases the mother is at the top of the hierarchy, but not necessarily so.[10]

Multiple caregiving often has been associated with discontinuous and inadequate caregiving, which is generally assumed to be harmful. In Yarrow's infant study, approximately forty percent of the middle class sample of one hundred had had "multiple primary caregivers or had several changes in caregivers during the first six months of life." Yarrow states that:

> There is a possibility that warm
> primary mothering associated with
> some discontinuity may not be de-
> trimental to the child. In fact
> it may help the infant to become
> more adaptable....We may have under-
> estimated the infant's capacity to
> form strong attachments to several
> adults.[11]

Ainsworth concurs with the potential value of
multiple attachments. She states that although

> it seems certain that too many
> potential attachment figures may
> mitigate against the formation of
> any attachment to anyone, the evi-
> dence does not necessarily suggest
> that it is essential or even optimal
> for mother and child to form an ex-
> clusive dyad.[12]

Ainsworth continues: "A spreading of attachment relationships over several figures may be healthy and may,
under some circumstances, prove to be highly adap-
tive."[13]

Studies of children reared in Kibbutzim are frequently cited in connection with the subject of multiple mothering. The Kibbutz child lives in a communal
setting with primary caretaking provided by a variety
of child nurses—called metapelets. Although "the
biological mother usually is available for feedings
during the first months of life, her presence is not
continuous"[14] (she lives elsewhere), and after the
first six months or so the mother typically returns to
work and parental visiting of the child is usually
limited to an hour or two a day. (Emphasis mine.) Rabin
stated: "After the first several months, the role of the
mother and the amount of contact with her infant dimin-
ishes. At the same time, the role of the metapelet becomes increasingly important."[15] The philosophy of
child rearing in the Kibbutz transfers the control and
responsibility of children from the family unit to that
of the community as a whole."[16]

Rabin compared randomly selected Kibbutz and non-
Kibbutz individuals of different age groups in terms of

social maturity and general development as assessed via scales, tests and projective techniques. Rabin concluded that

> Multiple mothering, as it is practiced in the Kibbutz, despite some minor temporary difficulties and effects on the early developmental pattern, has no long-range deleterious effects on personality development and character structure.[17]

Rabin describes a less intense relationship of Kibbutz children with their parents. Identification with the same-sex parent is not strong, and cathexes (e.g., bonds) to peers more prevalent than in our society. Yonina Talmon states that "solidarity in the Kibbutz is focused primarily on horizontal ties among age peers rather than on vertical ties among successive generations."[19]

Talmon's evaluation of the parent-child relationship stresses the importance of this tie, even though "parents do not carry the main responsibility for either maintenance or socialization of their children."[20] Talmon indicates that the emphasis in the relationship is on the affective nature of the tie. "Parents endeavour to make the few hours that their children spend with them as pleasant and carefree as possible.... The main function of the parents is to minister to their children's need for security and love."[21]

Maccoby and Feldman compared American and Kibbutz reared children in regard to mother-attachment and stranger reactions. They found few significant differences between the two groups in spite of distinctively different methods of child rearing. In a discussion of their findings, Maccoby and Feldman state their conclusion that it is "the quality rather than the quantity of mothering (which is) of (primary) importance in the development and maintenance of attachment."[22] They also suggest that while "interaction between mother and child is important, the sheer availability of the mother is not."[23]

Certainly there is an enormous difference between a home-reared American child who receives multiple

141

caretaking because his parents work, and a communally-reared Kibbutz child who receives multiple caretaking because it is the prevailing cultural pattern. Any generalizations or predictions from one society to another based on one factor alone—i.e., multiple caretaking—risk oversimplification. Thus, while it might be reassuring for working parents to know that Kibbutz children form meaningful attachments to their parents even in the face of very little time spent together, it cannot be assumed that an analogous situation would necessarily prevail here. A striking difference in the two situations is the fact that American parents who work outside the home continue to have many home-based responsibilities. The kind of idyllic situation described by Talmon of being able to focus <u>exclusively</u> on the child during the few hours of parent-child contacts simply does not exist for American working parents.

However, as we have already indicated, the research related to parent-child attachment and multiple caretaking leads toward the same general conclusions as the Kibbutz studies: absence of measurable emotional problems associated with multiple caretaking, and no indication of defects of the parent-child attachment relationship.

In our own study we noted a broadening preference for non-parental caretakers among the older four and five-year-olds. This is consonant with the older child's expanding social interests, which welcomes interactions beyond the family circle, while still retaining strong parental attachments. There is no reason to cling to the idea of exclusive parental caretaking as a desirable model, even if circumstances permitted it. The normal thrust of the child's growth and development is toward expanding relationships. This growth is most facilitated when the child has diverse opportunities to interact with non-parental caretakers.

A quote from Freud (1910) conveys his endorsement on theoretical grounds of the widening sphere of the child's attachment relationships:

> It is inevitable and perfectly normal that a child should take his parents as the first objects of his love. But his libido should not remain fixated on these first objects;

later on it should merely take them
as a model, and should make a gradual
transition from them on to extraneous
people when the time for the final
choice of object arrives. The de-
tachment of the child from his parents is thus a task that cannot be
evaded if the young individual's
social fitness is not to be en-
dangered.[24]

Of course the age at which this task occurs is a critical issue which we will discuss later in this chapter.

In summary, we have identified the following potential advantages for the young child in multiple caretaking experiences:

1. Increased opportunities for multiple
   attachments
2. Increased opportunities for development of peer bonds
3. Promotion of the child's natural
   developmental thrust toward wider
   social contacts
4. Avoidance of "over-dependence" on
   parents

We will now consider the topic of independence as
it relates to preschool children and their progression
toward self-reliant coping.

Moving Toward an Independent Stance. The widening
circle of contacts beyond the family offers a natural
progression from the total dependence of the infant to
the mutual interdependence and reciprocity of adult
relationships. In between these two states are the
fiercely independent stances often found during ado-
lescence and also during the later preschool years.
The four and five-year-old child has a strong wish to
do things for him or herself in many situations. We
saw numerous examples of children refusing help when it
was offered because they so desperately wanted to perform a particular task themselves (e.g., blowing up the
balloon which we gave them during our first visit, or
opening up the box of cupcakes brought for desert at
the dinner observation visit).

Erik Erikson considers the major development task of the four and five-year-old child as the resolution of the conflict between initiative and guilt.[25] Hence the young child's refusal of help often stems from his or her strong need to take the initiative in order to demonstrate his new ability. In Erikson's view, the curiosity and persistence of the Oedipal child (ages three to six) often elicits restraining, impatient, or shaming responses from caretaking adults, resulting in the development of guilt reactions in the child and the beginning formation of the conscience or super-ego. Although the caretakers may have reservations about the young child's "I can lick the world" cocky confidence, this does not usually diminish the child's natural thrust toward self-sufficiency and "independence." The wish to cope independently without adult ministrations came through poignantly in some of the study children's projective stories. Three examples follow.

### Children's Stories: "Hurt" Situation

### Name of Child: Scott

R: "This is a different story. The boy is playing on his rocking horse. And he is rocking so hard that he falls off, and he hurts his leg, and he's starting to cry."

C: And he, and then he goes to the hospital.

R: Who takes him to the hospital?

C: His Mommy.

R: And they go to the hospital, and what happens in the hospital?

C: (Pause.) He gets a bandage on him.

R: And then does he feel better?

C: Yes.

R: And then what do they do?

C: The Mommy puts him in a wheel car.

R: You mean a wheel chair?

C: Yeah.

R: And does she wheel him out the door?

C: No. He wheeled hisself.

R: Oh! I bet he likes to do that. And then what?

C: And then he didn't feel better. He.... it just hurted still.

R: So what's going to happen?

C: They're gonna hafta take both of those bones that broke out, and put another new one in.
R: They are? They're going to have to do a big operation? The poor little kid! So he's going to have to stay in the hospital, huh?
C: For a few days.
R: Is he still crying? He must be kind of unhappy and sad.

C: Yeah.
R: And then what? What about the rest of his family? Do they know about it?
C: No.
R: Just the Mommy. Is she going to stay there with him?
C: No.
R: She's going to go home? And he's going to stay in the hospital all by himself?
C: Yes.
R: And then what's going to happen?
C: He's going to feel better.
R: Oh good. You mean that after they do the operation he's going to be all better? That's good.

Comment: Note C's insistance that he wheel himself in the wheel chair and his structuring the story so that the child remains alone in the hospital.


Name of Child: Elizabeth

R: "The little girl is going to play on the rocking horse, etc. She falls down, and she hurts herself. She's starting to cry because it hurts so bad. Now you tell me what happens next."
C: Her Mommy comes along.
R: And what does Mommy say?
C: Mommy says that she has to go to the doctor.
R: So is the Mommy going to take her right away to the doctor?
C: Yes. Where's the car?

R: We have to pretend we have a car. Let's
pretend that this is the car. Now they're
going to go in the car.
C: She hurt her eye.
R: Oh! Is she still crying?
C: Yes.
R: And is the doctor going to help her?
And make her feel better?
C: And the Mommy's going out.
R: And Mommy's going with her?
C: No! (emphasis) The Mommy's going out
to take a walk. This little girl's going
to have a patch on her eye.
R: Her right eye. And then will she be
better after a while?
C: Yes.
R: OK. Now, let's make up another story.

Comment: This story is very similar to that
of the previous child's insofar as the mother
leaves the hurt child in both instances. It
is impossible to evaluate whether the children
in either instance have, in reality, felt
abandoned by their mothers when they were hurt
or ill, or whether their fantasied episodes
reflect their struggles with the independence/
initiative issue.

A third child's story about the same "Hurt" theme
calls forth a similar self-sufficient response.

Name of Child: Walter

R: "The little boy is rocking on his rock-
ing horse, and he rocks so hard that he
falls off, and hurts his leg. He's
starting to cry because it hurts so much.
What happens next? You finish the story."
C: He calls the doctor.
R: By himself?
C: Yeah.
R: Does he know the doctor's telephone
number?
C: Yeah.
R: He calls him up by himself and what
does he say?
C: He say: 'I'll be right over.'
R: And then what does the little boy do?
C: Then he fixed his leg and no more boo-boo.

146

```
R:   And what does the Mommy do?
C:   She makes cook.
R:   And what does the Daddy do?
C:   He watching TV.
R:   And what does the Gramma do?
C:   She's reading the paper.
R:   OK.  And that's the end of the story?
C:   Yeah.
```

**Comment:**  We are quite convinced that the parents of the children in the above examples never would have abandoned them in real life if, in fact, they had been hurt or injured. It seems plausible to us, however, that these children whose working parents certainly have not **always** been on the scene in situations where the child was hurt, have learned that they can, if necessary, cope and survive without their parents' comfort or involvement.  This is further illustrated in the folloiwng example.

**Observation Visit:**  Extended Family
                       Excerpt Related to "Hurt"
                       Situation
**Name of Child:**  Ronald

   (GF=Grandfather; GM=Grandmother)

During this visit which occurred following a backyard barbecue on Father's Day, GF asked C to tell R about how he hurt his eye when he visited them.  C told R he went to the doctor and got stitches, but "they are all gone now."
GM to R:  "He didn't even cry.  He is such a trooper."

**Bedtime Visit:**  Two Weeks Later
                    Excerpt Related to "Hurt"
                    Situation
**Name of Child:**  Ronald

M was in the process of putting C's younger twin siblings to bed.  C was playing, dressed in his pajamas, in the living room.  Since R knew one of the siblings had been in the

hospital for a tonsilectomy the previous
week, R mentioned this to C and asked if
he had ever been in the hospital.
C to R:    "I was once.  I had to get two
              stitches in my eyelid."
M came into the room as C was saying this.
M to C:    "Ronald, you have a terrific
              memory.  I wouldn't have even
              remembered those stitches if
              Mrs. Webb had asked me that
              question."
C to M:    "That's because _you_ weren't there
              when it happened!"

These examples from the children's stories and real
life situations suggest that several of our study children coped courageously and effectively with their parents' absence, even in situations where they were physically hurt.  Denial of the need for help from the attachment figure at a time of stress such as physical
injury is unusual behavior, and by no means typical of
the majority of the children in this study, most of whom
indicated a strong preference for their mothers when
they were hurt (Questionnaires, Observations and Projective Stories).

These reported instances of "self-reliant" and/or
"independent" behavior (both real and imagined) demonstrate the pull toward initiative/independence in some
preschool children whose self-image includes the ability
and/or wish to behave autonomously in difficult situations.

It is likely that children, like adults, have unrealized potential strengths which emerge in response
to the demands of a particular situation.  The absence
of the primary attachment figure may predispose the
child to more independence-type behavior.  This subject
merits further study in terms of the influence of parental absence on children's coping behavior, including
problem solving and autonomy.

Seeking Proximity for Help and for Affection.  We have
discussed proximity-seeking as an indicator of attachment, and need to clarify this in terms of the child's
independence-type behavior, which in many respects seems
antithetical to the desire to be close to a particular
person in certain situations.

Proximity-seeking can be considered to have two main purposes—one, the obtaining of needed help or assistance, and the other, the quest for physical and emotional gratification. The first purpose while not restricted to attachment figures, tends to be oppposed by the older preschooler's push for independence.

The study children were frequently spontaneously described as "independent," especially by their grand-mothers and, as we have noted, several of the children's own projective stories stressed this independence theme. This was illustrated in both Scott's and Elizabeth's stories about being alone either in the hospital or with the doctor when hurt, and in Walter's story when the child called the doctor himself when hurt, and in John's story in which the child gets his own oatmeal in the morning, and finds his family in the zoo by himself when he is lost. (Latter example from Doll Play Story.)

It might be argued that these reactions are percep-tions or feelings of the children based on the fact that since both parents work and are frequently away the chil-dren feel that they can't rely on anybody and have to fend for themselves. It is possible that this might be part of the rationale behind these stories. Perhaps, the stories enable the child to experience a sense of mastery and increased self-confidence. However, in view of the children's frequent refusal of help even when it was available, we consider this behavior more as reflect-ing the child's desire to do something him or herself or not do it at all—a kind of stubborn independence. Prox-imity-seeking for the purpose of getting help or assist-ance is often resisted by the older preschooler who has a strong wish to do things for himself and to enhance his own self-sufficiency. When the child does request help, this may be solicited from anyone. Hence, prox-imity - seeking for obtaining help is not selective enough to be a valid indicator of attachment.

Proximity-seeking for the purpose of physical and emotional gratification, however, is quite different. This can be considered a valid indicator of attachment, especially when it is person and situation specific. Children are not at all reluctant to express their wishes for "affectionate and comforting behaviors" in their ob-served and projected interactions with their caretakers. When Steven was tripped by his brother and fell and hurt his arm, he went immediately to his mother for comfort, and when Louis' father was sitting at the dinner table eating, Louis came up behind him, climbed up the back of the ladder-back chair and spontaneously planted a kiss on his father's cheek. Stories before bedtime are usually read either with the child in the caretaker's lap, or with the caretaker lying down beside the child on the bed. Children very much enjoy this form of proximity and will initiate it themselves if the caretaker does not do so.

Direct verbal expressions of positive regard (e.g., "I love you") were very rare among the study children, but behavioral expressions of attachment were common. There were numerous instances (some rather fleeting, albeit clear) of what seemed to be affectionate, "loving" contact between the child and various caretakers—a quick hug, a pat on the head, and (especially) extended lap-sitting and cuddling before bedtime. The lack of direct verbal expressions of affection may reflect the difficulty of many people, both adults and children, in putting their feelings into words.

Maintaining continuous contact with an attachment figure is not necessary for the older preschooler, but he or she very clearly may want and expect certain contact behaviors—"observable affectionate and comforting behaviors"—at certain times. Thus, while the frequency with which proximity-seeking contact behaviors may diminish with age, the form in which attachment relationships are expressed continues to be in a behavioral (proximal) mode involving close physical contact between the child and the attachment figure. This behavior can be directed toward a teacher (Kathy), or toward a sitter (Elizabeth); however, the parents tend to be the primary focus of this proximity-seeking behavior.

Timing of Maternal Separation. Since the children in this study had mothers who were currently or who had been working or in school for a large part of the children's lives, we examined the issue of maternal separation in relation to its potential effect on attachment formation. If there is an optimal time or sensitive period of maternal and infant bonding, as some researchers suggest,[26] then the mother who is away from home is not as readily available as a potential attachment figure as is the substitute caretaker who assumes responsibility for the child in the mother's absence.

Separation of the child and mother is a complicated situation with many variables contributing to the impact of the experience. The present study focused mainly on current relationships rather than on the child's reactions to past separations which had been precipitated by mother's involvement in work or school. Some parents and teachers gave information spontaneously, however, when a separation experience had been difficult or traumatic for the child. Five of the study children experienced separation problems of varying degrees, according to spontaneous reports of parents and teachers. These children were: Elizabeth (at age eight months), Cindy (at age thirty-six months), Kathy (at age thirty-six months), James (at age sixty months), and Scott (at age thirty-six months).

With the exception of Elizabeth, the rest of these children had experienced separation from their mothers at a later age than the majority of the study children whose mothers went to work during the first year of their lives. Cindy and James both had experienced little multiple caretaking prior to their mothers' decisions to enroll them in day care at age three, so that the mothers could attend college. Cindy's mother stated that Cindy had cried every day for a year when she began day care! The following year she did not cry and, in fact, assumed a "mothering," comforting role with children new to the Center whom she appeared to take under her wing. James, who had a similar caretaking history, had difficulty adjusting to a change of day care at age five when he was transferred from a Center where he had been enrolled for two years and where he had evidently formed a strong "attachment" to his teacher, according to his mother, (Discussed in Chapter Three). It is likely that the transfer to a different Center represented a traumatic breach of the attachment bond which James had formed to his teacher.

A similar break in an important relationship plus a change in physical setting contributed to Kathy's unhappiness when she entered day care. (Although Kathy had adjusted well in the private caretaking arrangement with one regular sitter from the time she was eighteen months, her entrance into day care at age three proved to be so traumatic she cried every day for two weeks when her parents left her there.)

Changes in the mother's work schedule can also create unanticipated negative responses from children. Scott had been in day care for about six months, and, in addition, was cared for by both parents who divided housekeeping and child care responsibilities evenly. When Scott's mother switched from part time to full time work, Scott began to protest being left at day care. His mother thinks he may have been reacting to her reduced time with him (his protests diminished after a month or so).

Elizabeth's separation problem at age eight months also seemed to be related to a change in her mother's work schedule. The mother added a part-time teaching job to her other part-time position in a bank, and a new sitter was engaged to care for Elizabeth during the additional hours mother was away. Mother recalls Elizabeth crying every time she left her with the college sitter, although she evidently didn't cry on the days she was with the other (familiar) sitter. Mother decided "it wasn't worth the hassle," and she gave up this job after one semester. Since stranger-anxiety often occurs at age eight months, this is generally a poor time to introduce a <u>new</u> caretaker. Elizabeth had evidently formed an attachment to the other caretaker, and did not object to being left by mother with this familiar sitter, but could not tolerate the introduction of a new caretaker at this particular time of her life.

We looked for life-history factors in common among the five children who were reported to have experienced traumatic entry into or resistance to day care. Examination of the children's experiences revealed the following commonalities: 1) <u>few regular sitters prior to entry to day care</u>, and 2) <u>no prior group experiences</u>, such as informal neighborhood play groups or half day nursery programs prior to entry to day care. It seemed that for these children staying home with the mother, or one other caretaker, did not provide the child with an adequate <u>range</u> of experience for dealing with the diversity subsequently encountered in the day care setting. We presume that these children who had trouble adjusting to day care had strong attachments to their parents, and we believe that their life experiences had not provided them with the reassurance of knowing that non-parental caretakers could also meet their

152

needs and provide security and love. Margaret Mead's previously quoted statement bears repetition here:

> Cross-cultural studies suggest
> that adjustment is most facili-
> tated if the child is cared for
> by many warm, friendly people.[27]

While conclusions based on five children are only suggestive, at least two factors seem to have contributed to these particular instances of separation anxiety. The factors are:

1. the <u>age of child</u> when repeated maternal separations occurred, and
2. the <u>child's prior caretaking experiences</u>

Since one of the primary goals of qualitative research is to generate hypotheses which can more fully be explored and tested in future research, we present the following propositions about the timing of maternal separation, based on our very small sample, and recognizing the need for verification with a larger population of children of working parents.

1. Maternal separation on a regular basis as occurs when the mother embarks on a routine of work or school is more traumatic to the child when it occurs <u>after twenty-four months of age</u>, particularly <u>when there have been few other regular caretakers</u> with whom the child has had experience prior to that time.

2. Maternal separation (as above) is more traumatic when the child is placed directly into a group care situation, without prior experience with multiple caretakers in the child's or sitter's home, or without prior group experience with peers, such as a neighborhood play group or half-day nursery school.

<u>Implications</u>. We believe that children <u>benefit</u> from the experience of care by non-parental caretakers. Therefore, it makes sense to encourage the use of sitters and/or other substitute caretakers <u>early</u> in the child's life when he or she is prone to form attachments and to accept substitute care (three to eight

months of age). We have noted that children who have not had early extra-familial caretaking may have considerable difficulties adjusting to day care at a later date (age three).

Similarly, some group experience seems to be helpful prior to enrollment in day care. Mothers of young children should therefore consider the informal neighborhood play group, or the half-day nursery school program as potentially beneficial to their child in providing good preparation for later full time day care. The goal is to broaden the childs' security system to include a number of potentially helpful adults, to some of whom he or she may become attached. The notion of "innoculation" against separation anxiety by early multiple caretaking experiences is one of the noteworthy findings of our study.

Many children experience separation anxiety in the process of leaving the security and familiarity of parental care and entering an unknown environment, surrounded by unfamiliar children and entrusted to the care of strange adults. In fact, a child who rushed eagerly into such an experience without any hesitation would be unusual and cause concern among knowledgeable child development specialists. There is a difference, however, between initial wariness which gradually subsides as the situation becomes familiar, and the extreme protest of severe separation anxiety, which permits no consolation for a prolonged period of time.

It is important for day care personnel to know the child's caretaking history prior to entry into their program, and to plan to integrate the child gradually, if he or she has had little prior experience with nonparental caretakers or with small groups prior to enrollment. Parents, also, need to understand that their child's past experience is important in terms of the opportunities it provided for exposure to new people and settings. The child who has experienced adults other than the parents as benevolent caregivers has learned an important lesson for future relationships with an expanding social network.

NOTES

1. Murphy, Lois, _The Widening World of Childhood_ (New York: Basic Books) 1962.

2. Lasch, Christopher, _The Culture of Narcissism_ (New York: Warner Books) 1979).

3. Winn, Marie, "What Became of Childhood Innocence?", _The New York Times Magazine_, January 25, 1981.

4. See, for example, Aries, Philippe, _Centuries of Childhood: A Social History of Family Life_ (New York: Vintage Books) 1962 and Shorter, Edward, _The Making of the Modern Family_ (New York: Basic Books) 1975.

5. Kotelchuck, Milton, "The Nature of the Child's Tie to His Father, " Ph.D. Dissertation, Harvard University, 1972.

6. Lamb, Michael, _The Role of the Father in Child Development_ (New York: John Wiley & Sons) 1976.

7. Schaffer, H. Rudolph and Emerson, Peggy, "The Development of Social Attachments in Infancy," _Monographs of the Society for Research in Child Development_, Serial No. 94, Vol. 29, no. 3, 1964.

8. Yarrow, Leon, "The Development of Focused Relationships During Infancy," _The Exceptional Infant_ Vol. 1 in _The Normal Infant_, J. Hellmuth, ed. (Seattle: Special Child Publications) 1967.

9. Schaffer and Emerson, op. cit., p. 71.

10. Ibid., p. 197.

11. Yarrow, Leon, _Infant and Environment: Early Cognitive and Motivational Development_ (New York: John Wiley & Sons) 1975, p. 171.

12. Ainsworth, Mary, "The Development of Infant-Mother Attachment" in _Review of Child Development Research 3_, Bettye Caldwell, ed. (Chicago: University of Chicago Press) 1973, pp. 1-94.

13. Ibid.

14. Rabin, A. I., _Growing Up in the Kibbutz_ (New York: Springer Publishing) 1965, p. 107.

15. Ibid.

16. Ibid., p. 9.

17. Ibid., p. 210.

18. Ibid., pp. 211-214.

19. Talmon, Yonina, _Family and Community in the Kibbutz_ (Cambridge: Harvard Press) 1972, p. 28.

20. Ibid., p. 24.

21. Ibid.

22. Maccoby, Eleanor and Feldman, Shirley, _Mother Attachment and Stranger Reactions in the Third Year of Life_, Monographs of the Society for Research in Child Development 37 (1, Serial No. 146), 1972, p. 81.

23. Ibid., p. 82.

24. Freud, Sigmund, _Five Lectures on Psychoanalysis_ The Standard Edition, Vol. 11 (London: Hogarth) 1953, originally published in 1910.

25. Erikson, Erik, "Identity and the Life Cycle," _Psychological Issues_, Vol. 1 (New York: International Universities Press, Inc.) 1959, pp. 74-82.

26. Klaus, Marshall and Kennell, John, _Maternal-Infant Bonding_ (St. Louis, Mo.: C. V. Mosby Co.) 1976.

27. Mead, Margaret, "Some Theoretical Considerations on the Problem of Mother-Child Separation," _American Journal of Orthopsychiatry_ 24 (July 1954), p. 477.

# Chapter Nine

## SOCIALIZATION FOR LIFE IN A SOCIAL WORLD

> "It is likely that a society, what-
> ever its conscious intentions, more
> or less inevitably produces a method
> of upbringing whose crises and dif-
> ficulties, as well as its assets,
> contribute to the development of human
> beings adapted to that society."[1]

This quote reflects both the limitation and the challenge implied in the socialization process. A blunt way of rephrasing it would be to say that we get what we socialize for, even though we may not conscious-ly be aware of our goals. Rapaport states further that

> All societies will pay a price—
> a necessary sacrifice—in the coin
> of developmental crises and path-
> ology, for their successes in adapt-
> ing their successive generations to
> their ways of life. The educational
> goal of any society is to perpetuate
> its way of life and ideals.[2]

Socialization has been defined as "the process by means of which an individual is integrated into his society."[3] While the family traditionally is the ini-tial and primary socializing agent of the young child, other societal institutions such as school, community and church organizations have always also shared this responsibility.

Robert LeVine sees parents as the primary media-tors between the environment and their children.[4] He lists three elements as intrinsic to the socialization process: 1) "enculturation, or the intergenerational transmission of culture, 2) the acquisition of impulse control, and 3) role-training or training for social participation."[5] Reciprocity between the individual and the social system is also an important aspect of socialization.

> Whatever its role demands, the
> social system must allow individu-
> als sufficient satisfaction of their
> intrapsychic needs; and whatever
> their press for satisfaction, indi-
> viduals must perform appropriately
> in their social roles.[6]

Sociologists Frederick Elkin and Gerald Handel
define socialization as "learning the ways of any established and continuing group."[7] They believe that
"socialization begins with personal attachment, specifically in the mother-child relationship."[8] (emphasis
mine) This evolves later into the child's perception
of significant other individuals as role models and
identification figures. The socialization process
which typically begins at home in the mother-child relationship, then expands to the school setting, where
the child becomes "linked to a wider social order,"[9]
according to Elkin and Handel.

The child who attends day care as a preschooler
receives socialization influences from at least two
sources—the family and the day care center. The
effects of such dual socialization would seem to depend
at least partly on the extent to which values and expectations in the home and day care center are similar
or different. Anthropologists stress the plasticity
of human nature, yet there clearly are limits to the
degree to which the young child can assimilate conflicting demands and incompatible expectations. Probably many parents are at least marginally aware of this
when selecting a day care program, or other regular care
situation for their children. Parents usually visit a
program, talk with other mothers, or have their own ways
of "checking out" various child care alternatives in
their attempt to choose an arrangement which supports
their own values as far as possible.

Socialization from multiple sources is inevitable
as the child grows older, with most child development
specialists viewing this as a positive force. Favez-
Boutonier, for example, recognizes that although the
preschool program can not replace the family group, it
can provide a "complementary means of apprenticeship
to social life."[10] Burton stresses the importance of

peer group exposure as providing important extra-familial influences on the child:

> The peer group does act as a powerful socializing agent in rewarding and censuring and successfully shaping the behavior of its members in conformity with group standards.[11]

Children of working mothers automatically receive socialization from multiple extra-familial sources: other caretakers (both related and non-related) child care personnel in day care and nursery programs, unrelated sitters, peers, and neighbors. We would not expect the child to form attachment bonds to all those with whom he or she has a caretaking (socializing) relationship. However, these extra-familial contacts offer opportunities for the development of selected attachment bonds, in addition to providing a broad base of socialization.

Our world, and that of our children, is changing very quickly. Mothers of young children are leaving home to go to work in unprecedented numbers and they expect their young children to accept and adapt to substitute caretakers. The evidence suggests that the children, for the most part, are adapting with the impressive ease of childhood flexibility. The parents of these children, however, have not all caught up with them. Many parents hold values of the generation in which they were raised, in which most mothers stayed home; this was not only expected, but also revered behavior. These values produce the guilt of the working mother, so well recognized by day care professionals, by social workers and other mental health practitioners who have contact with young families. The ingrained value that mothers of young children belong at home is now threatened by social and economic reality which as yet lacks a value system supportive of this reality.

Perhaps we can learn from another culture. The opening up of China to American visitors in the 1970's has revealed a totally different pattern of child care which might, at least in part, have some application here. Ruth Sidel, an American social worker who visited China in 1971 and who subsequently wrote Women and Child Care in China, states that "the Chinese are attempting to fashion a human being who will put the needs

of the society before his own."[12]   As in the Kibbutzim,
the Chinese merge the goals of the individual with
those of the group, and their socialization system is
the epitome of this unified purpose.

In modern China children from a very young age
receive multiple mothering.  Fifty-six days after a
baby's birth his or her mother returns to work, and
the baby typically receives care from an "auntie" (unrelated caretaker) in a nursing room at the mother's
place of employment.  This arrangement permits the
mother to remain in frequent contact with her child
at the workplace where she may breast feed her baby
for a year and a half, while simultaneously involved
in employment herself.  After age one-and-a-half until
age three, the child usually is cared for in a nursery
apart from mother's place of employment or at home by
a grandmother or other caretaker.  Eighty percent of
children in urban areas between the ages of three and
seven are involved in such "kindergarten" programs,
according to Ruth Sidel.

Since the ultimate aim in China is that the individual have multiple allegiances—to his family, his
work, his Mao Tse-tung study group, his party, his
local revolutionary committee, his city or commune, a
set of ideas, and to China herself—multiple mothering
in early childhood facilitates the child's comfort with
groups and with a variety of relationships.[13]  The
Chinese encourage their children to engage in various
forms of "mutual help" from a very early age.  They
teach ideological, revolutionary concepts and ideals
as soon as the child has the rudiments of understanding.
The Chinese proverb-slogan typifies the all-pervading
communal spirit:  "If we are not as cement, we shall be
as sand."[14]

American culture does not aspire to this extent of
uniformity and conformity.  In fact, we value our diversity and our individuality.  However, the Chinese pattern of child care demonstrates a socialization model
which includes non-parental caretakers, without weaken-
ing of family bonds in spite of the extensive non-parental caretaking.

Erik Erikson refers to "the responsibility of each
individual for the potentialities of all generations,
and of all generations for each individual."[15]  This

ideal of mutual responsibility, like the Chinese system
of child rearing, directs our attention beyond the
mother-child dyad, focusing instead on the social milieu
and surrounding culture group. The notion of reciprocity is an important influence binding one generation
to another.

With increasing numbers of working parents pass-
ing young children into the arms and laps of numerous
subsidiary caretakers, our society needs to re-evaluate
the potential meaning of this experience for the child.
The low status and wages of child care workers in day
care centers clearly devalues the very vital function
they perform.

Our children live in a world with multiple caretakers, and thus far the research evidence, including
this study, suggests that this is beneficial to them.
The reality of today's world reflects Bruno Bettleheim's
thinking, based on his study of Kibbutz children:

> For the ego, for the personality
> to develop, the infant needs to
> experience satisfaction and chal-
> lenge at his own pace. But nowhere
> has it been demonstrated that for
> survival, or mental health the
> satisfactions, challenges, and frus-
> trations must all originate in the
> same person.[16]

Uri Bronfenbrenner, in a testimony before the
Senate sub-committee on Children and Youth in 1973 expressed concern about "withdrawal of adults from the
lives of children" due to increased numbers of working
mothers, increase in divorce and reduction of the number of adults in the family.[17] While it may be true
that children receive care less frequently from relatives, the boundaries of the child's caretaking circle
are actually stretching to include non-related caretakers, many of whom may come to have a significant
impact on the child's life.

Our society has yet to develop, but clearly needs,
subsidiary child care programs which are neighborhood-
based and staffed at least partly by retired or unem-
ployed local citizens. Bronfenbrenner suggested the
location of day care centers in or near public schools

so that older children could get some experience caring for the young. A sense of "community" child care responsibility could beneficially replace the isolated nuclear family concept. Elizabeth Kubler-Ross has suggested the juxtaposition of day care centers and senior citizen centers, where both generations would benefit from intermittent contact with the other.[18]

The family residence as the necessary site for the cradle and playpen made sense when mother was home baking bread and darning socks. Moving the young infant to the mother's place of employment (as could be done if day care were available at the work site) and/or developing locales for child care in the child's neighborhood are both practical responses to the need for child care in view of the fact that the house is empty.

We need to endorse the concept of shared socialization of the young child as a value consistent with the reality of working parents, and ultimately advantageous to the child, and to society. Parents will never be _replaced_ by other caretakers, since the parent-child relationship is unique, but they certainly can be _assisted_, and this assistance promises to enhance all the participants.

Growing up with working parents in the 1980's translates into growing up with a network of diverse caretakers in a variety of settings. This involvement gives the young child a backlog of valuable experiences and the opportunity to form multiple attachments and peer bonds. Our contemporary world prizes both individuality and group compatability. Meaningful involvement with a wide social network in childhood initiates and prepares the child to function comfortably in a world which encompasses many significant spheres beyond the nuclear family.

NOTES

1. Rapaport, David, "The Study of Kibbutz Education and Its Bearing on the Theory of Development," _American Journal of Orthopsychiatry_, 28:3, 1958, p. 596.

2. Ibid., p. 597.

3. Honigman, John, <u>Handbook of Social and Cultural Anthropology</u> (Chicago: Rand McNally) 1973, p. 1101.

4. LeVine, Robert, <u>Culture, Behavior and Personality</u> (Chicago: Aldine) 1973, p. 62.

5. Ibid.

6. Ibid., p. 66.

7. Elkin, Frederick and Handel, Gerald, <u>The Child and Society</u>, 2nd ed. (New York: Random House) 1972, p. 6.

8. Ibid., p. 37.

9. Ibid., p. 111.

10. Favez-Boutonier, J., "Group Influences on Personality Development" in <u>Mental Health and Infant Development</u>, K. Soddy, ed. (New York: Basic Books) 1956, p. 138.

11. Burton, R., "Psychological Aspects of Socialization," <u>Encyclopedia of Social Sciences</u> (New York: Collier) 1968, p. 542.

12. Sidel, Ruth, <u>Women and Child Care in China</u> (Baltimore: Penguin) 1973, p. 82.

13. Ibid., p. 105.

14. Ibid., p. 126.

15. Erikson, Erik, <u>Insight and Responsibility</u> (New York: Norton) 1964, p. 157.

16. Bettleheim, Bruno, <u>The Children of the Dream</u> (New York: Avon) 1970, p. 211.

17. Bronfenbrenner, Urie, "The Origins of Alienation," <u>Scientific American</u>, August 1974.

18. Kubler-Ross, Elizabeth, E-T-V Program, November, 1975.

# EPILOGUE

## SUMMARY AND IMPLICATIONS FOR FUTURE RESEARCH

The study on which this book is based supports Bowlby's theory of primary attachment and develops and advances this theory to a new level by analyzing the nature of the parent-child relationship which endures with special significance despite the reduced time of working parents for interactions with their children.

We suggest that the unique presence of <u>three types of parental behaviors</u> contribute to the development and persistence of strong attachment bonds. We found these behaviors to be typical in parent-child interactions, and rare in the child's contacts with other caretakers. It remains for future research to further test these indicators of attachment with a larger population of children.

The parental behaviors we identified as unique, are as follows:

1. <u>Unsolicited Impingement</u> of the parent on the child ("nudging" and "bugging"): see pages 85-92.
2. Use of <u>"Pet Names"</u> (Nick names): see pages 101-104.
3. <u>Idiosyncratic Interactions:</u> see pages 104-108.

Measures for assessing the presence of these behaviors, appropriate for use with a larger sample need to be developed, since the method used in the present study (the color coding of extensive field notes) would be impractical for large-scale use. As mentioned previously, the use of pet names and the rituals of idiosyncratic interactions both tend to be private behaviors, of which the parents, themselves, may not be fully aware. The behaviors become evident in repeated home-based observations of an observer who is sensitive to recurring modes of address and patterns of interactive behaviors. Some form of observational check list could be developed to capture and tally these unique interactions.

An additional study finding, that of the preference of the study children for their grandmothers over
their sitters, despite the less active involvement of
the former, suggests the ability of the young child to
pick up cues regarding their importance to their grandparents. Although the grandparents in our study did
not usually engage in the impinging behaviors typical
of the study parents, they did frequently have affectionate pet names for their grandchildren, and clearly
communicated their special status to them.

These findings, together with the notion of
"innoculating" children against separation anxiety
experiences, point strongly to the importance of the
parent-child (and grandparent-child) bond. These
are primary relationships, which do not diminish in
the face of repeated work-related separations. Multiple caretaking adds to the child's network of relationships, without eroding the primary attachment bond between parents and their children.

Study Limitations. Our research was based on an original sample of nineteen families, with seventeen completing the full course of observation visits, questionnaire responses, and projective play interviews.
Since we intended to probe the nature of the attachment relationships of older preschool children, we
chose to study a small group in an intensive way. We
wished to generate hypotheses which could subsequently
be tested with a larger sample in future research.

Our small sample makes no pretense of being typical. We did not use a control group, so do not know
about the relationships of children whose mothers do
not work outside the home. We were not interested,
at present, in comparing children of working parents
with children of parents who are home. Rather, we
wished to focus on the range and nature of the attachment relationships among a small group of children,
whose parents both work.

These aims, which initially seemed both modest and
feasible, at times during the research seemed elusive
and difficult to illuminate. We believe, however,
that the contribution of our work rests in our analysis
and interpretation of some of the unique aspects of the
parent-child bond, which ultimately serves as the pro-
tocal for all attachment relationships.

## APPENDIXES

1. Original Doll Play Stories

2. Questionnaires

   Caretaker Questionnaire
   Teacher Questionnaire

3. Letter to Parents

4. Child Study Home Visit Plan

5. Summary of Content of Child's Drawings

6. Coding Guide for Observational Field Notes

# ORIGINAL DOLL PLAY STORIES

**Introduction:** "We're going to play with some dolls and make up some stories about the dolls. Would you like to help me finish some stories I already started about these dolls? The tape recorder machine will make a record of our voices so I can put our stories in my book." (Five minute exploration of the recording machine.)
"Let's start the stories now. I'll begin a story, and you tell me how it finishes."

## 1. Play-Recreation

The first story begins on a Sunday afternoon. Everybody in the family is home. (Researcher will introduce fami-dolls which correspond to child's own family.) Here is the Mommy and the Daddy, the Girl/Boy, Brother/Sister, etc. (If appropriate): The Grandmother/Grandfather, Aunt/Uncle are visiting. The Girl/Boy (corresponding to sex of child) doesn't have anything to do. She/he wants somebody to play with her/him. What happens next?

## 2. Hurt

This is a different story. The Boy/Girl is having a lot of fun playing on the rocking horse. The mother is in the kitchen making lunch. The father is watching TV. Grandmother/Grandfather is looking at a magazine. All of a sudden the Boy/Girl begins to rock harder and harder and suddenly he/she falls off the horse, and hurts her/his leg. He/she begins to cry. It hurts a lot! What happens next?

## 3. Nurturance

Everybody just came in the house for dinner. They are all very hungry. Everybody is in the kitchen together. The Boy/Girl says he/she is starving. "I want a glass of milk, please!" What happens next?

> What does the Mommy say?
> What does the Daddy say?
> What does Gramma say?
> Etc. (naming all dolls involved in play episode)

The Boy/Girl can sit next to anybody he/she wants at the table. Who does (s)he sit next to? Who is on the other side?

## 4. Bedtime

It's getting close to bedtime. The Boy/Girl is tired
and sleepy. Mommy, Daddy and (Gramma, Grandfather,
etc.) are all sitting in the living room watching TV.
The Boy/Girl is yawning; he/she is _so_ sleepy. What
happens next?

## 5. Fear (Separation)

The family is going on a trip to the zoo. The whole
family is together, and everyone is happy because
they are going to have a good time watching the ani-
mals. Here is the Boy/Girl, and the Mommy and the
Daddy and the Gramma/Grandpa. Now they are all in the
zoo. They are watching the monkeys swinging in the
cage. The Boy/Girl loves to watch the monkeys because
they are so funny. The Boy/Girl is watching the monkeys so much that he/she didn't see the rest of the
family going to the next building to see the lions.
The Boy/Girl is left by him/herself. All of a sudden
he/she finds out that her family is not with him/her.
He/she doesn't know where they are. He/she is getting
afraid. What happens next?

## 6. Original

Now you can make up your very own story about the
family if you want to. You can make them do or say
anything you want.

CARETAKER QUESTIONNAIRE:
CHILD STUDY RESEARCH PROJECT

Researcher:
(Mrs.) Nancy Webb, M.S.S.
Doctoral Student
Columbia University

Identification No:_____

Date: _____

Please check your relationship to the child: Brother___
Sister___Grandmother___Grandfather___Uncle___Aunt___
Cousin___Sitter___Other___

Length of time you have known the child: Since birth___
Other (describe)_____

EXPLANATION: This questionnaire is about the child's
typical behavior, according to your opinion. There
are no right or wrong answers. Please supply the
answer which is most typical of the "average" week.
If you don't know the answer you may leave it blank.
Your responses will be considered confidential and
will not be shared with anyone. The child's parents
have given consent to this Research project.

How frequently do you see the child in the average
week?_____

When you are caring for the child, who does he or she
talk about the most among the family circle and regular caretakers?_____

Among the family circle and regular caretakers, who do
you think the child is closest to?_____

Does the child like to hug and kiss? A lot___Some-
..times___Rarely___
Does the child like to sit on your lap? A lot___
  Sometimes___Rarely___
Does the child have strong preferences regarding who
⁺ takes care of him/her? Yes___No___ If Yes, please
  name the person _____

171

Are there any special activities the child wants to
engage in with you, rather than with anyone else?
Yes___No___ What?_____

When you are caring for him/her, does s/he usually play
alone?___Play with other children? With Brother?___
With Sister?___Other? (Who?)_____

Does s/he come to you and try to get you involved in
his activities? Sometimes___Frequently___Rarely____
Never___

How would you describe the child's relationship to you?
Exceptionally close___Warm and friendly___
Casual/indifferent___Not friendly, and sometimes
hostile___

How would you describe this child's typical manner of
interacting with caretakers? Demanding, wants a lot
of attention___Seems to crave affection___Rarely asks
for help___Shy, withdrawn___Other_____

Please list anything which usually frightens the child
Dogs___Other animals___Lightning___Loud Noises___
Dark___ Other _____

If child is frightened, who does s/he go to for comfort? Father___Mother___Grandmother___Grandfather___
Sitter___Anyone___

Think of the last time the child was hurt or sick.
Who does he/she want with him when s/he is hurt or
sick? Mother___Father___Sister___Brother___
Grandmother___Sitter___Grandfather___Other___
Anyone___

How do you get him to stop crying when he hurts himself? Holding___Kissing___Talking___Singing___
Band-aid___Other(describe)_____

Are there times when you cannot soothe the child by
any means when he is crying? Frequently can't___
Sometimes can't___Usually can___Always can___

If you can't, do you think someone else could? Yes___
No___ If Yes, Who?_____

Do you think the child is affectionate? Yes___No___
Less than I'd like___More than necessary___About
average___

Does the child talk about the adults who take care of
him at the day care center? Yes___No___Rarely___
Sometimes___Frequently___

Is the child especially fond of any one particular
person at the Center? Yes___No___ If Yes, please
give name of person_____

Anything about the child's relationship with you or
  with other people that might be important for
  Researcher to know about?_____

_____

Thank you for your impressions. Please do not discuss
the questionnaire with the child's other relatives or
caretakers, since they will be asked some similar questions. All your answers are confidential. No names
or identifying information will be used in the final
research report.

                        Thank you again.

                        Researcher: Mrs. Nancy Webb

TEACHER QUESTIONNAIRE:
CHILD STUDY RESEARCH PROJECT

Name of Child: _____

Name of Teacher: _____  Date: _____

<u>EXPLANATION</u>: This questionnaire is intended to supple-
ment the Researcher's observations. Its purpose is to
explore the child's <u>typical</u> social interaction pattern
in the Day Care setting. Please answer in terms of the
child's "average" behavior. Your responses will be
considered confidential, and will not be shared with
the child's family, nor with other Day Care personnel
in your Center. Names will be removed from the form
by the Researcher, and replaced by an identification
code number to insure confidentiality. The child's
parent(s) have given consent to this Research Project.

Length of time you have known the child_____
Approx. no. of hours per day you spend at Center_____
What are your typical work hours? _____

How would you describe the child's relationship to you?
   Exceptionally close___Warm and friendly___Casual/
   Indifferent___Not friendly, and sometimes hostile___

With how many adults at the Center does the child have
   regular contact?_____
Does the child seem to prefer any one adult caretaker
   at the Center? Yes___No___  If Yes, Who?_____
   Any ideas as to the reasons behind this preference
   (if Yes)?_____
   _____

How would you describe this child's typical manner of
   interacting with adult caretakers? Demanding, wants
   a lot of attention___Seems to crave affection___
   Rarely asks for help___Shy, withdrawn___Other___

If child is hurt, what does he/she usually do? _____
_____
Does he/she go to one person in particular for comfort?
   Yes___No___  If Yes, Who?_____

175

How can he/she be soothed when s/he gets hurt?
  Holding___Kissing___Talking___Band-aid___
  Singing___Other___

If child is afraid, what does he/she usually do? _____

_____
Does he/she go to one person more than others for comfort?  Yes___No___    If Yes, Who?_____

If child had his choice, which adult would he/she prefer to sit next to at lunch time, in your opinion?

_____

Do you think the child is affectionate?  Yes___No___
  About average___More than average___Less than
  average___
Does the child like to sit on your lap? Yes___No___
  Rarely___Sometimes___A lot___
Does the child like to hug and kiss?  Yes___No___
  Rarely___Sometimes___A lot___

Does the child talk about his parents and/or other
  people at home?  Yes___No___Rarely___Sometimes___
  Frequently___
Whom does he talk about the most?  Mother___Father___
  Relative___Sitter___Other (specify)_____

How would you describe your over-all feelings toward
  this child?  Positive___Neutral___Negative___

Anything about the child's relationship with you or
  with other people at the Center that might be important for Researcher to know about? _____

_____

Thank you for your impressions.  No names or identifying information will be used in the final research
report.

                    Researcher:
                    (Mrs.) Nancy Webb, MS.S., A.C.S.W.
                    Doctoral student
                    Columbia University
                    School of Social Work

## LETTER TO PARENTS

Typed on Official Day Care Center stationery, and
signed by the Director. Center will distribute letters to selected families, who will independently return the form to Nancy Webb in the envelopes provided
by her.

---

March   , 1978

Dear _____ :

Mrs. Nancy Webb, a professional Social Worker, is currently doing research for her doctoral degree at Columbia University. Mrs. Webb is researching early childhood development, day care, and typical behavior of
four and five year old children.

She would like to visit some of our parents in their
homes to discuss her study. You don't have to participate, of course; but I think you might find it interesting, and hope you will be willing to talk with her
about it.

The Center Board of Trustees has voted its approal of
this project. We have agreed to cooperate with Mrs.
Webb because we feel that her study will add to scientific knowledge about children.

If you would like to participate, please use the form
below. (Mrs. Webb has assured us that your participation will be held in the strictest confidence.)

If you have any questions about this, please call me.

                       Sincerely,

                       Name of Director
                       Title

---

Please tear off and return in the enclosed envelope.

Yes, I am willing to talk with Mrs. Webb about her study.

Telephone No.         Name: _____
                      Address: _____

# CHILD STUDY HOME VISIT PLAN

(Note: This Plan was discussed with parents during the first visit, and then left with them, for their future reference during the ongoing course of the study.)

Since meal times, bedtimes and the comings and goings of various family members are important occasions in a young child's life, I would like to be present at various times when these events are occurring. The outline and summary below describe the visiting schedule I would like to plan for the next few weeks. All visits will be planned in advance at your convenience.

It will be desirable to complete the visits within a month—its theoretically possible to finish in ten days and many families may find it convenient to do this. In the case of sickness, bad weather or conflicting plans the visits can be re-scheduled, and the interval will be longer. Since the researcher wants your child to gradually get to know her, it isn't sensible to space the visits too widely.

| Situation | Approx. Length of Visit | Date | Persons Present |
|---|---|---|---|
| 1. Weekend afternoon | 1 hour | Today | Entire Family |
| 2. Pick-up at Day Care and Family Dinner | 2 hours | | Entire Family |
| 3. Parent(s)' Afternoon Out | 1 hour | | Relative/Sitter Parent(s) arrive home during R's visit |
| 4. Parent(s)' Night Out | 1 hour | | Relative/Sitter Parent(s) leave after R arrives |
| 5. Bedtime | 1 hour | | Entire Family |

# CHILD STUDY HOME VISIT PLAN
## (continued)

1. Introduction and explanation of study.
   Parent(s) fill out questionnaire.

2. Researcher will be at Day Care Center when
   child is picked up.
   Researcher will return home and observe child
   during Family Dinner.
   Researcher will bring dessert.

3. Researcher will arrive during time child is
   being cared for by relative or sitter. Plan
   is to observe child for about one-half hour
   before parent(s) return home, and about one-
   half hour after.

4. Similar to above, except that Researcher will
   arrive approximately one-half hour before par-
   ent(s) plan to leave the house, and she will
   remain about one-half hour after they leave.

5. Concluding visit. Gift for child. Researcher
   would like to observe child's usual bedtime
   routine.

SUMMARY OF CONTENT
OF CHILD'S DRAWINGS


No: _____

Total No. of Drawings: ____

I.  Family Content

    Who is the most important person to the child?

        Drawn largest?
        Drawn with most detail?
        Positioned closest to child?

    Is family pet included?

    Are extended family members included?


II.  Non-Family Content

    Subjects:

        Researcher
        Other (list)

    Objects (specify)

# CODING GUIDE FOR OBSERVATIONAL FIELD NOTES

| Item Coded | Color |
|---|---|
| **I. Individuals** | |
| Mother/Father | Red |
| Relative | Green |
| Sitter/Researcher | Brown |
| **II. Type of Interaction** | |
| Open displays of emotion | Blue |
|   Positive = + | |
|   Negative = - | |
| Child initiates interaction | Orange |
| Child protests separation | Pink |
| Child responds to caretaker | Yellow/Green |
| Caretaker responds to child | Turquoise |
| Caretaker initiates inter-<br>action | Purple |
| **III. Mode of Interaction\*** | |
| Verbal Interaction | Black |
| Behavioral Interaction | Yellow |

\***Note:** It is recognized that these categories overlap with the others above. In instances where more than one category applies these are coded twice by indicating a "V" or "B" (to designate "verbal" or "behavioral" interaction) above the more specifically color-coded item.

# BIBLIOGRAPHY

AINSWORTH, MARY, "Attachment and Dependency: A Comparison," in Attachment and Dependency, ed. J. Gerwirtz, Washington, D.C.: Winston, 1972.

AINSWORTH, MARY and WITTIG, B., "Attachment and Exploratory Behavior of One-Year-Olds in a Strange Situation," in Determinants of Infant Behavior IV, ed. B. Foss, New York: Wiley, 1969.

AINSWORTH, MARY, "The Development of Infant-Mother Attachment," in Review of Child Development Research, Vol. 3, ed. Bettye Caldwell, Chicago: University of Chicago Press, 1973.

ARIES, PHILIPPE, Centuries of Childhood: A Social History of Family Life, New York: Vintage Books, 1962.

BANE, MARY JO et. al., "Child-care arrangements of working parents," Monthly Labor Review, October 1979.

BANE, MARY JO, Here to Stay: American Families in the Twentieth Century, New York: Basic Books, 1976.

BERNARD, JESSIE, The Future of Motherhood, New York: Penguin Books, 1974.

BETTLEHEIM, BRUNO, The Children of the Dream, New York: Avon, 1970.

BOWLBY, JOHN, Attachment and Loss, Vol. 1: Attachment, New York: Pelican, 1969.

BOWLBY, JOHN, "The Nature of the Child's Tie to His Mother," International Journal of Psycho-Analysis, 39, 1958: 350-373.

BRAZELTON, T. BERRY, "Early Parent-Infant Reciprocity," in The Family: Can It be Saved? Victor Vaughan, III and T. Berry Brazelton, eds. Year Book Medical Publishers, Inc., 1976.

BRONFENBRENNER, URIE, "Encounters of the Third Kind," Second Annual Lucille Austin Memorial Address, Columbia University School of Social Work, April 20, 1981.

BRONFENBRENNER, URIE, "The Origins of Alienation," Scientific American, August 1974.

BURTON, R., "Psychological Aspects of Socialization," Enclyclopedia of Social Sciences, New York: Collier, 1968.

COLLINS, GLENN, "Friendship: A Fact of Life for Toddlers, Too," The New York Times, December 15, 1980.

DAVIS, MINNIE, Ideal Motherhood, Boston: Crowell, 1898.

DI LEO, JOSEPH, Children's Drawings as Diagnostic Aids, New York: Brunner/Mazel, 1973.

ELKIN, FREDERICK and HANDEL, GERALD, The Child and Society, 2nd ed., New York: Random House, 1972.

ERIKSON, ERIK, "Identity and the Life Cycle," Psychological Issues, Vol. 1, New York: International Universities Press, Inc., 1959.

ERIKSON, ERIK, Insight and Responsibility, New York: Norton, 1964.

FAVEZ-BOUTONIER, J., "Group Influences on Personality Development," in Mental Health and Infant Development, K. Soddy, ed., New York: Basic Books, 1956.

FREUD, SIGMUND, An Outline of Psychoanalysis, London Hogarth, 1938.

FREUD, SIGMUND, Five Lectures on Psychoanalysis, The Standard Edition, Vol. 11, London: Hogarth, 1953, originally published in 1910.

FRAIBERG, SELMA, Every Child's Birthright: In Defense of Mothering, New York: Basic Books, 1977.

FRAIBERG, SELMA, "The Origin of Human Bonds," Commentary, December, 1969.

GESELL, ARNOLD and ILG, FRANCES, Child Development, New York: Harper Bros., 1949.

HARLOW, HARRY, Learning to Love, New York: Ballantine Books, 1971.

HENRY, JULES, Pathways to Madness, New York: Random House, 1971.

HINDE, ROBERT, "On Describing Relationships," Journal of Child Psychology and Psychiatry 17, 1976: 7.

HOFFMAN, LOIS, "Effects of Maternal Employment on the Child—A Review of the Research," Developmental Psychology, 10, 1974.

HONIGMAN, JOHN, Handbook of Social and Cultural Anthropology, Chicago: Rand McNally, 1973.

KAMERMAN, SHEILA B., Parenting in an Unresponsive Society, New York: The Free Press, 1980.

KLAUS, MARSHALL and KENNELL, JOHN, Maternal-Infant Bonding, St. Louis: The C. V. Mosby Co., 1976.

KOTELCHUCK, MILTON, "The Nature of the Child's Tie to His Father," Ph.D. Dissertation, Harvard University, 1972.

LAMB, MICHAEL, "A Defense of the Concept of Attachment," Human Development, 17, 1974.

LAMB, MICHAEL, "Maternal Employment and Child Develop" ment," in M. E. Lamb (ed.) Nontraditional Families: Parenting and Child Development, Hillsdale, N.J.: L. Erlbaum Assoc., 1982.

LAMB, MICHAEL, The Role of the Father in Child Development, New York: John Wiley & Sons, 1976.

LASCH, CHRISTOPHER, The Culture of Narcissism, New York: Warner Books, 1979.

LeVINE, ROBERT, Culture, Behavior and Personality, Chicago: Aldine, 1973.

MACCOBY, ELEANOR and FELDMAN, SHIRLEY, Mother Attachment and Stranger Reactions in the Third Year of Life, Monographs of the Society for Research in Child Development 37, 1, Serial No. 146, 1972.

MEAD, MARGARET, A Cultural Anthropologist's Approach to Maternal Deprivation," Deprivation of Maternal Care, ed. Mary Ainsworth, Geneva, WHO, 1962.

MEAD, MARGARET, Blackberry Winter, New York: Morrow, 1972.

MEAD, MARGARET, "Some Theoretical Considerations on the Problem of Mother-Child Separation," American Journal of Orthopsychiatry 24, July 1954.

MEHL, LEWIS E. and PETERSON, GAIL H., "Spontaneous Peer Psychotherapy in a Day Care Setting: A Case Report," American Journal of Orthopsychiatry, 51:2, April 1981.

MINUCHIN, SALVATORE, et. al., Families of the Slums, New York: Basic Books, 1969.

MORGAN, JANE, O'NEILL, CHRISTOPHER and HARRÉ, ROM, Nicknames: Their Origins and Social Consequences, London: Routledge & Kegan Paul, 1979.

MURPHY, LOIS, The Widening World of Childhood, New York: Basic Books, 1962.

RABIN, A. E., Growing Up in the Kibbutz, New York: Springer Publishing, 1965.

RAPAPORT, DAVID, "The Study of Kibbutz Education and Its Bearing on the Theory of Development," American Journal of Orthopsychiatry, 28:3, 1958.

ROWE, MARY, "Choosing Child Care: Many Options," in Working Couples, eds. Robert and Rhona Rapaport, New York: Harper Colophon, 1978.

RUBIN, ZICK, Children's Friendships, Cambridge, Mass.: Harvard University Press, 1980.

RUTTER, MICHAEL, Maternal Deprivation Reassessed, Baltimore: Penguin Books, 1972.

RUTTER, MICHAEL, "Social-Emotional Consequences of Day Care for Preschool Children," American Journal of Orthopsychiatry, 51:1, January 1981.

SALK, LEE, Preparing for Parenthood, New York: David McKay, 1974.

SCHAFFER, H. RUDOLPH, "Some Issues for Research in the Study of Attachment Behavior," in Determinants of Infant Behavior II, ed. by B. Foss, New York: John Wiley & Sons, 1963.

SCHAFFER, H. RUDOLPH and EMERSON, PEGGY, "The Development of Social Attachments in Infancy," Monographs of the Society for Research in Child Development, Serial No. 94, Vol. 29, no. 3, 1964.

SHAPIRO, THEODORE, Discussion: "Problems of Mother-Infant Bonding," Conference on Contemporary Issues in Child Mental Health Practice, New York Foundling Hospital, New York, June 3, 1981.

SHORTER, EDWARD, The Making of the Modern Family, New York: Basic Books, 1975.

SIDEL, RUTH, Women and Child Care in China, Baltimore: Penguin, 1973.

SLATER, PHILIP, The Pursuit of Loneliness, Boston: Beacon Press, 1970.

SOLNIT, ALFRED J. and STARK, M. H., "Mourning and the Birth of a Defective Child," Psychoanalytic Study of the Child, 16, 1961: 523-537.

SMITH, ROBERT P., Where Did You Go? Out. What Did You Do? Nothing. New York: Norton, 1968, ed. reproduction of 1958.

SURVEY RESEARCH CENTER, "Summary of United States Time Use Summary," Mimeo, Ann Arbor, Michigan, University of Michigan, 1966.

TALMON, YONINA, Family and Community in the Kibbutz, Cambridge: Harvard Press, 1972.

THOMAS, ALEXANDER and CHESS, STELLA, Temperament and Development, New York: Brunner/Mazel Publishers, 1977.

UNCO, National Child Consumer Study: 1975, Vol. 2, Washington, D.C.: U.S. Department of Health, Education and Welfare, Office of Child Development, prepared under contract #105-74-1107, 1976.

WEBB, NANCY BOYD, Attachment Relationships of Preschoolers to Parents and Other Familiar Caretakers: Implications for Day Care and Working Mothers, (Unpublished doctoral dissertation, Columbia University School of Social Work, New York, 1979, Ann Arbor, MI: University Microfilms.

WHITE, STEPHEN L., "Family Dinner Time: A Focus for Gathering Family History," Master's Thesis, Smith College School for Social Work, Northampton, Mass., 1974.

WHITING, BEATRICE, ed. Six Cultures—Studies of Child Rearing, New York: John Wiley & Sons, 1963.

WHITING, BEATRICE, "The American Family: A Cross Cultural Perspective," presentation, Harvard Alumni College, Cambridge, Mass., July 11, 1978.

WINN, MARIE, "What Became of Childhood Innocence?", The New York Times Magazine, January 25, 1981.

WOODWARD, KENNETH and KORNHABER, ARTHUR, "Where Have All the Grandparents Gone?" The New York Times, May 10, 1981

WOODWARD, KENNETH and KORNHABER, ARTHUR, Grandparents/ Grandchildren: The Vital Connection, Garden City, New York: Doubleday, 1981.

YARROW, LEON, Infant and Environment: Early Cognitive and Motivational Development, New York: John Wiley & Sons, 1975.

YARROW, LEON, "The Development of Focused Relationships During Infancy," in The Exceptional Infant, Vol. 1: The Normal Infant, ed. by J. Hellmuth, Seattle: Special Child Publications, 1967.

YARROW, MARION, et. al., "Child rearing in families of working and non-working mothers," Sociometry 25, 1962.

ZIGLER, EDWARD F. and GORDON, EDMUND W., eds. Day Care, Boston: Auburn House Publishing Co., 1982.

193